A Life in Liturgy: Rediscovering the Mass

A pioneer liturgist tells of the success, problems, and challenges of the liturgical renewal

to Fr. Phil, with my esteem. Joe Nolan

by

Rev. Joseph T. Nolan

Acknowledgements:

Scripture quotations are from The New Revised Standard Version of the Bible, copyright 1989 by the Division of Christian Education of the National Council of the Churches of Christ in the USA.
Used by permission. All rights reserved.

Readers may contact the author, Joseph T. Nolan, at nolanj@bc.edu.

ISBN: 978-0-615-18172-1

Cover design: Jonathan Gullery
Printed by RJ Communications, New York, NY, 10017

This book is gratefully dedicated to

Rev. William J. Leonard, S.J.
Rev. Shawn Sheehan
Rev. Frederick McManus
Rev. Thomas Carroll
Rev. Joseph Collins
Dr. Theodore Marier

They loved the prayer of the Church.

Contents

CRITIQUES OF LITURGICAL REFORM

SUGGESTIONS AND THE FUTURE

THE FUTURE OF LITURGICAL RENEWAL

Preface

I offer this book to those who love the liturgy, especially the Mass, and would like to know more about it, especially their part in offering it.

The reform of the liturgy, made official in 1962 with the Vatican II document *Sacrosanctum Concilium*, and the reform of the Mass, made official in 1970 by Pope Pius VI, had their origin in the Liturgical Movement, which began in the 19th century in Europe. It is rare that a movement succeeds so well in achieving its objective. The reform has not satisfied everyone: I reflect in the text on the tension and problems that remain, and offer suggestions both large and small to continue the renewal. I do so because I have loved my role as a priest these many years, baptizing, teaching and preaching, marrying, sending the beloved to God, and above all, offering the Mass with people.

But why another book when scholarly works on the liturgy abound? I know they do; I have read them and taught the subject. They are often difficult going; it is the usual way .of scholars, and I present many of their conclusions in easier prose. But I also add my own insights and experience. As a lay person I was drawn into the Liturgical Movement through the example of an extraordinary group of priests in the Boston area to whom I dedicate this book, along with a layman, Theodore Marier. The priests had various assignments: teaching, canon law, pastoring, chaplaincy in war, ministry to the blind, etc. Over and through it all was an exciting commitment to liturgical renewal; they had read the books and "walked the talk." It was not easy to break this new ground; liturgists were pilloried as "litniks" and told they should be Benedictine monks. Indeed the Benedictines, especially from St. John's Abbey in Collegeville, Minnesota, as well as Conception Abbey in Missouri and St. Meinrad's in Indiana, were untiring leaders in the movement. My friends and mentors brought the Liturgical Conference to Boston in 1948, and it was a thrilling time of prayer, ideas new and old, a promised reform that would within two decades be officially realized. But not without much unfinished business, such as vernacular translations, new approaches to confession – now the sacrament of reconciliation – architectural changes to church buildings, the placing of a table altar with the priest facing the people, and the involvement of lay people in what hitherto had been strictly priestly work and privilege. Not least was the biblical revolution that produced a new lectionary. The return to the vernacular. And a reform of the Divine Office. We were called to become, far more than before, a biblical people who prayed together in the great prayer of the church. And also, called to recognize the dignity of our baptism, a call to lay people to participate in liturgy which was really an expression of their share in Christ's priesthood.

This revolution (or restoration) in the way we pray had been well prepared for over a century. But a change of this magnitude inevitably ran into problems. The book faces these but also the successes: a people praying the Mass, appreciating their baptism, more assured of the resurrection (the Easter Vigil, the changes in the funeral liturgy), and much more. In the fall of 2005 I asked a class of older people who were taking my course in adult Catholicism to give their opinion on all this. I was surprised at how much satisfaction was expressed that people now actually participate in the Mass. One woman said, "I never thought I would see women around the altar except to change the altar linens or rearrange the flowers; now they read the scriptures and help give out the communion." She found this a revolution. It is. The look of any Catholic Mass is now strikingly different from 1962 and the previous four centuries. But it is also wonderfully the same, especially the sense of the Real Presence. Even the complications of language did not dismay my friends; some loved and wished for more of the Latin, but others said they could identify with the actions of the Mass anywhere, in any language.

I begin with my personal story because I think it is important to experience Mass, as I did, in every possible scene, and also to know a little of what lay life is like. Fresh out of Boston College I applied and joined the Federal Bureau of Investigation. Yes, the FBI. It had a stellar reputation in those days. After months in fingerprint analysis I moved on to agents training at Quantico, Virginia, and was sent for my first assignment as a special agent to Little Rock, Arkansas and the field office of Fort Smith. I liked this work. It was efficient, power was used with restraint, and it was an important part of the war effort. In the Ozark hills it also proved to be dangerous; I had adventures there that I usually tell only in a party atmosphere! But I recall also my feelings as a Catholic layman; on the train to Fort Smith I sat next to a Catholic priest who answered my questions about a Catholic church, saying that there were three – one in the center of town, usually called the Irish church, another one called the German church, and a third on the outskirts of town, for the black people. Then he remembered a fourth, Christ the King (which I presume welcomed everyone!).

Two years into the war the Bureau "invited" all its younger agents to seek a commission in the armed forces, and mine – as an ensign in the naval reserve – arrived in the mail. The only requirement was to sign the oath in the presence of a naval officer. The Naval Intelligence chap visited regularly, came in and said – "Sign here." But I insisted on assembling the whole Little Rock office, taking the oath with flag in hand, etc. (ritual, yes). In Washington, friends had a party for my "investiture" in an officer's uniform. Subsequent assignments led me to Brazil, a communications school at Harvard, and a long overseas stay in the Philippines. It was there in Manila that I reunited with Fr. Bill Leonard, an Army chaplain who recounts all that in two of his own memoirs. My interest in the Mass was constant and involved me in giving a radio commentary for Manila on the Christmas midnight Mass at the naval base.

I returned to the FBI, to the New York office this time, and relished the assignment because I could renew an old acquaintance with the Catholic Worker. The FBI had a file on them – of course, because anyone who worked with the poor and were "radicals" were also suspected Communists. But it was a "dead file," marked "no evidence of subversion." Dorothy Day greeted me for the second time – now a friendly FBI agent and before that a naval officer – and she said, with dry humor, "You really are a creature of the state!" Many years later, three years before her death, I celebrated Mass in Los Angeles in an upstairs chapel of the Sisters of Social Service. They have been a remarkable group ahead of all the reform of the sisterhoods and the liturgy. Influenced by Benedictines, they drew their spiritual formation from the church year. The main chapel had a bible enthroned at the entrance, until (this is hard to believe) an auxiliary bishop ordered it removed because all that "looked too Protestant." Shortly before the Mass they told me that Dorothy would be there. It was the feast of St. Augustine and I tried to recall, without a copy, his great sacramental prayer that begins, "What do I love when I love Thee?" She told me afterwards how much she loved that passage, and would send it to me. In teaching undergraduates, her famed autobiography, *The Long Loneliness*, was always part of the course.

Dorothy Day really understood so much about the church – its prayer life, the devotions, the Mass and liturgical year, the saints, the mystical tradition, the implication of the liturgy for a true brother- sisterhood, the social teachings of the church, and – what else? The need for an institution, the organized church, although she was an unfailing critic of it.

While going to college I did other things to survive, such as drive a lunch truck and climb around the framework of the battleship *Massachusetts* under construction, work in a restaurant and a hotel, deliver mail at Christmastime. I also worked one summer on a farm, actually ploughed with a horse and milked cows. As a pastor I tried to understand and share as much as possible the lives of my parishioners, visiting where they worked, sharing their family life. It led me to the conclusion that the sacrifices a priest is called upon to make – and the most difficult is giving up marriage and family – are less by far than married people make in raising a family.

So the book that follows is autobiographical and then becomes doctrinal. We need in-depth discussion of what liturgy, especially the Mass, really is, and can become for ourselves.

Joseph T. Nolan
Boston College
Easter, 2007

LITURGICAL JOURNEY

The Making of a Liturgist

I am sometimes asked how it all began – the priesthood, and my interest in the liturgy and preaching. There is never a single answer but I think back to a blazing August day and the Washington Mall, the nation's lawn which stretches from the Lincoln Memorial to the Washington Monument. Ten thousand of us are sitting on the grass at an outdoor Mass. We are Boy Scouts attending a national jamboree. The preacher is an archbishop, and he is droning on. And on. Something like an airplane in a holding pattern. And you are just dying to have him land, and get it over with. It was a great occasion and of course he had prepared The Great Address. I am fifteen. And I am thinking two things: why do they do this? And, I can do better than that.

I have had that experience often, reflecting on the irrationality of what is done supposedly for our benefit – giving a sermon to which no one is really listening, and in which the only hope aroused is the hope that it will end. Driving east from Kansas one time during a major shift in my life, heading to Harvard University and a new life of the mind, I listened on the radio to the installation of an archbishop (another one).

When it was his turn to preach I found myself smothered by a blanket of religious language. That happens when passages of scripture, and not much else, are quoted with a certain unction; nothing of the human condition, no particularity, nothing of flesh and blood, passion or life, enters the discourse. Again, two things occurred to me. (1) This man is reasonably healthy – good perhaps for 15 or 20 years. (2) Being a prelate, no one will ever tell him the truth, at least about his preaching style. They may tell him the truth about diocesan finances, but not about his preaching. So we are going to hear this – or turn it off – for a very long time.

There were other, more positive influences. A kindling of the flame in college happened because I went to Mass – everyone did, in those days – and a priest there named William J. Leonard was interested in something called the Dialogue Mass. The people recited the server's part, taking over from the altar boy and adding prayers like the Gloria and the Credo. Actually all this was called the *Missa Recitata,* because you wouldn't dare to do it in English, not even if the priest did his thing in Latin at the same time (that kind of dual Mass came later). All this Latin participation was facilitated by a red, white, and black booklet with the Latin printed for dialogue. It replaced the rosary or prayer book with which pious Catholics usually occupied themselves while the priest went about his holy business. The booklet was authored by Fr. Gerald Ellard, S.J., another of a suspicious breed called Jesuit liturgists. Both he and Leonard were my guides in this "new" but very old spirituality. Ellard had written a book, well-researched and readable, called *Christian Life and Worship.* It was enormously useful in opening up, at least in the midwest where it was widely read and used in college courses, the themes of what was coming to be called the Liturgical Movement.

The first dialogue Mass at Boston College (in Latin, remember) was a bold step. Here we were in a small Gothic chapel, a group of pious students; I was the lector – a new and unheard of distinction, reading the epistle and the gospel while the priest read them *sotto voce,* and then leading the group in the prayers. It was dangerously close to upstaging the priest, or acting like one. And that's what we were afraid of. To give this Mass authenticity, Leonard had selected for the celebrant (or perhaps he couldn't avoid) a venerable Jesuit who looked like an angry Moses, shaking his white mane of hair and rumbling deeply at you. He preached retreats with saccharine stories and heartrending appeals to stay out of hell and to love God. Anyway, he knew about this "innovative" Mass and did not appear to disagree, but at the end of it he charged back to Fr. Leonard at the rear, who thought the worst was coming. "My boy, my boy," he said, "it carried me back to the day of ordination when I said the Mass together with the bishop!" (In the ordination rite that does happen - after the gospel, when the deacon becomes a newly anointed priest, he joins the bishop in offering what is really his first Mass.)

So the first *Missa Recitata* happened, and left what? Hardly an indelible mark, but I do remember it. In later years Fr. Leonard organized a summer school of liturgy at the college and got in Jesuit hot water because he gathered a few of us to sing Lauds. Jesuits were prepared in the Counter-Reformation period to be "in the saddle" or on the move, not monks in monasteries singing songs. The 150 psalms and a lot of other things were packed into four books called the *Breviary,* and after the Council of Trent all priests were required to read this ponderous prayer which the monks for centuries had gracefully sung (and still do). Now it became an hour of recitation that could be done anywhere and undoubtedly did move some to genuine prayer, although it was all in Latin. It didn't matter that the group Leonard had gathered were not Jesuits - it was just something Jesuits did not foster. You would think we were founding a monastery.

This awareness of the Mass as something prayed, not endured, as something more than an obligation, began to grow on me. Soon I acquired the *St. Andrew's Missal*, which came out of Collegeville, Minnesota and St. John's Abbey. It was a formidable book, presenting the whole liturgical year, all of the feasts and seasons and Sunday Masses in Latin and English. In fact, missals of every kind were beginning to multiply in the 1950s. The St. Andrew's did well with the liturgy but had a triumphalist history of the church throughout the centuries tucked into one of the opening essays. World War II brought about a leap forward in the "dialogue Masses." A remarkable priest from Brooklyn, Fr. Joseph Stedman, took a look at the ponderous bilingual missals and decided he could do better. And he did. He got out the first pocket missal, one for Sundays, one for every day in Lent. The one for Sunday was adopted by the armed forces and turned up in GI hands everywhere in World War II. It was clearly marked for people to take their part, and colorfully printed with excellent designs by Ade de Bethune. Liturgists found it somewhat cluttered with pious prayers and even touches of poor theology. But never mind; Fr. Stedman was a merchandiser, he saw a need, and answered it. You can still find his pocket missals in the collection of liturgical materials at Boston College, because the same Fr. Leonard became an archivist and collected everything that denoted piety and liturgy in those years of change.

I remember walking into a naval base in Recife, Brazil, seeking the Mass. I found it as the chaplain got up to say something like this: "I have to say this Mass in Latin, but you can say it with me in English. You have it right there in your pocket missal. So we both begin on page one. You just start and I'll make sure we stay together." Actually he threw in a few other remarks about the right of the people to participate, to know what's going on, to join in the prayer. No matter that he ignored the different roles, or any kind of rhythm to prayer; we just barreled along together, and right through the entire Mass, consecration and all. I think some shivered at the thought of these holy words coming from our unordained lips.

One of the slogans in those days was, "Don't pray at Mass, pray the Mass." That chaplain certainly believed it in his fashion. It became a fashionable cause to use the missal, and it could be overdone. In David Lodge's novel, *How Far Can You Go,* which is about young Catholics before and after the volcano we call the Second Vatican Council, he begins with a group at Mass at the University of London on a weekday in 1954. One of them, Hilary Bernard, is expertly whipping his ribbons (there were six of them, different colors) in the St. Andrew's missal from one part to another, ordinary to proper, saint of the day, special commemoration, etc. Like shifting gears in a high speed car. That happened in a novel but I recall people like that (and protest that I wasn't one myself). There is a story, probably true, about two maiden ladies, British to the core, who attended faithfully all the liturgical services, particularly during Holy Week. In those days, through a ghastly miscalculation of time that continued for centuries, the entire evening service called the Easter Vigil was carried out in the bright sunshine of Saturday morning. There was a high point to that interminable service which old timers are rightly nostalgic about. It was the intoning of the Gloria, accompanied by the ringing of the bells - every bell you could get your hands on. And the thundering answer of the choir, released from singing dull Lenten anthems at last, and free to come out with Alleluias. The visual side of this eruptive liturgy was the unveiling of the statues. All statues and crucifixes had been veiled or draped in purple for the previous two weeks. Now the coverings were removed, flowers were brought out, candles were lit. It was the Easter glory. And promptly at this moment, the two maiden ladies who had worn purple cloaks all week, rose solemnly and removed them, revealing their gowns of gleaming white satin underneath.

An experience in Milwaukee illustrates my state of mind about these things. I was still in a naval officer's uniform, and was there to visit Joe Dever and his young wife Margaret. They were living poorly but rich in hospitality, as the Irish so often are (Margaret was Welsh, but Joe was very much Irish), and I recall that we were going to have scrambled eggs for Friday supper. She stood at the stove stirring them while we talked and talked. Wonderful things to talk about. So much so that it was a long time before she discovered that she hadn't turned on the stove. The next day (after surviving the supper) I visited a huge, cavernous church called the Gesu, and if you know anything about Jesuits you can guess it was one of theirs. My intent was to go to confession. It was Saturday night, and that used to be a pious practice among Catholics. Leaving the church I met the sexton, an old man who was waiting for me to leave so he could lock up. I asked him if one of the Masses the next morning – Sunday morning – was a high Mass. High Mass, in the old liturgy, was sung all the way through and done with some solemnity. He said, "The eleven o'clock is, but it doesn't take any longer than the others, they have a fast priest." I'm sure he concluded that, like any other young, red-blooded American male, my motive in asking about the high Mass was to avoid it, certainly not to go to it. I had no great love of solemnity as such. I just felt that something important and profoundly significant was happening in any Mass and it should be treated in a serious, thoughtful fashion.

This carried over to sacraments. For the first time I began to go to baptisms as my friends married and had babies. It's hard to believe this now but baptism was very much a private ceremony in the past to which no one came. Well, somebody had to go and it was usually the godparents sent off with the newly born to get him or her plunged in the saving water and save the infant from a fate like Limbo (or maybe hell, according to earlier theologians). It was even considered unlucky in some ethnic groups for the mother to attend the baptism – I ran into that early in my priesthood and held up the ceremony until they went home and got her. The old attitude was that you simply went through the ritual and something called grace showered down on the infant; it was all done in Latin and with great dispatch.

The technical explanation for proceeding in this brisk fashion was something called *ex opere operato.* That meant the grace was given regardless of the quality or internal dispositions of the celebrant. It was a sheer gift from God that did not depend upon a gracious priest (or one in the state of grace). There certainly is a sound point to that but it also ignored a major statement of Thomas Aquinas that grace presupposes nature. Even God has to go through the medium of human beings, and if we act as if religious ceremonies are something just to get over, they are devalued, and people are quick to move on to something else. We have filled churches and emptied them, filled confessionals and emptied them in record speed under this misunderstood theology. The laity went right along with it and often spoke admiringly of their fast priest. One pastor on Long Island boasted about their "express Mass."

Later I would discover they spoke disparagingly of their slow priests. The challenge was to find a happy medium where such forgotten qualities as genuineness, meaning, and even enthusiasm or delight came through. In the early days of baptisms, because they were all in Latin (the ritual was not revised until 1958), I began to give explanations of the various symbolic actions. It's not good to get in too much of this habit; symbolic actions that have to be explained verbally are losing their power. But I was mostly concerned with language – a foreign tongue that obscured the beautiful sense of what was happening in christening a person. When at the Council of Trent the church froze the liturgy in the customary Latin, the French were among the first to use commentaries, and even publish them, to overcome this language barrier. I did not know of this precedent, and went ahead on my own to provide a "meaningful ceremony." Some of it worked; any fuss you made over their child was usually appreciated. For others, a timing mechanism in regard to church services was built in deeply - they just wanted to get it over with. That tribe is still around, even though their numbers do not increase.

The most bizarre example I heard of the speedup Mass was told to me about a largely Italian parish in the Northwest. The people were fully aware that when the priest reached what was then called "the last gospel" the Mass was almost over. And they came to life, which meant, for the women, opening and closing their pocketbooks to put away rosaries, prayer books, handkerchiefs, and what-not. The sound of the handbags opening and shutting came through like small arms fire, and prompted the priest to stop half-way through John's magnificent prologue (the "last gospel") and yell out, "Will you people *wait* a minute? Here I am up here trying to make time and you're not even polite enough to wait till I am finished." Trying to make time. So much for a gracious hour offered to God. (The Mass, of course, was closer to a half hour in those days.)

Right up to the reforms of Vatican II it was common to have the Sunday Masses on the hour, every hour, all through the morning. And the greatest charge laid upon the priest - I was warned very early – was certainly not one that exhorted him to preach the word, lead the worship, pray devoutly, encourage the people to lift up their hearts. Nothing of the kind. It was to clear the parking lot. This was the first commandment in the parish rule book. One Sunday when I despaired of racing the clock, with a long gospel that had to be read twice (once in Latin, then repeated in English), and frustrated with my determination to preach and preside at a Mass that did not resemble a verbal track meet, the older curate (we called them by that term then), a wise and funny Irishman, said to me, "You're right, of course. It is crazy. The apostles spent all their time getting them in, and we spend all our time getting them out." He was also the counselor who told me one day when I could not deal with the absurdity of some marriage case procedures or the obstacles that chancery offices put in the way, "You have to get used to the fact that in some places the church goes backwards." Later I would work this into a theology of salvation. It came down basically to the fact – very evident to me – that not even you nor I nor the church as represented in *some* parishes and by some priests can keep God from saving the people.

The black Mass. The "three priest Mass." These are all terms that are totally unfamiliar to later (post-reform) generations. The black Mass had nothing to do with diabolism; it was the Requiem Mass, and invariably the daily fare if you went to church on a weekday. For the half hour you were there, sometimes 15 or 20 minutes, it looked like a funeral. The priest was clad in black vestments; they were usually the cheapest and the oldest, well-worn (because they were worn so much) while the more expensive black and silver ones were saved for funerals. But what in God's name was happening on these weekdays? The Mass for the dead. The living were invited but the Mass was offered for this or that deceased person. This is still done because pastors refuse to do away with a system of stipends and intentions, but the point back then for a liturgist was that it destroyed all sense of the liturgical year, the feasts and seasons, the saints, the different gospels. The scriptures were read in Latin anyway, but the fare in the missal or the layman's book of the Mass (if he or she were odd enough to be interested) was simply ignored by the priest who was determined to say all these "special Mass intentions."

And why not, because he got the money. It was not dishonest; it was one reason he got a meager official salary - it was an attempt by the church to bind him to the service of the altar. If he needed money he simply had to stay around and offer a few

Masses. In medieval days there was a phenomenon called "the Massing priest" who was not quite chained to the altar, as some claim, but quickly ordained just to offer Masses for the dead on behalf of a family who retained him.

The Mass for the Dead was a votive Mass, which means one of choice or special focus, and the focus here was on the deceased and the Catholic belief that very probably they were in purgatory and you could help them with your prayers on the way to heaven. I do not mock this belief; like so many practices it developed as an answer to a human need, but I was dismayed at how close it came to selling the Mass or giving the appearance thereof. Shades of Martin Luther. Of course the money was called (and still is) an offering, and there is a strained effort by canonists to distinguish other "intentions" and "fruits of the Mass." But it was abundantly plain to the Olivettis or O'Briens that this was *their* Mass. The priest had better get the name straight and mention it out loud; by God, they had paid for it.

I said it destroyed the church year but of course no one paid attention to that except during Christmas, Lent, and Easter. And for ethnic groups, their favorite saint.

There were also features of the black Mass in some parishes which came close to outraging common sense, such as the mimicking or duplication of the catafalque. A catafalque is a sort of coffin on a stand, or a coffin containing the dead person, usually exposed, resting on a wooden structure appropriately draped and surrounded with huge, heavy candles. Popes are laid out this way in Saint Peter's square for the public funeral, and it can be impressive. But I was not prepared for what I ran into in mid-western parishes – a phony catafalque. It was something like two sawhorses and a couple of planks which were set up and taken down by the ever-willing or subservient altar boys. Upon it was placed a black wooden box – the coffin (without a body). The catafalque was draped with black velvet and the six yellow candles used only for funerals – very different from the chaste, white beeswax of other Masses – were placed around it. I hate to tell you this, but if you paid extra, you got the catafalque. Or perhaps it just went with a so-called "high Mass" in which the priest sang the prayers. He was not trained to sing and usually the results were far from melodious. But all this was done in the name of honoring the dead and collecting the stipends. In those days the stipend was five dollars for this musical prayer, and one dollar for a simple, plain, unadorned and, of course, much faster black Mass.

One day I could stand it no longer – it was some saint's day or a particularly appealing gospel I wanted to share – and I sallied forth courageously in vestments the color of the day (there are six "liturgical colors" spread throughout the feasts and seasons of the year). The pastor to his credit waited until I returned to the sacristy but then told me in no uncertain terms that deviations like this were not even remotely allowable. And he added, "Some day you'll be dead and be glad they are out there praying for you." I am sure he meant all this honestly; he was a devout, hard-working man. It was just a mercenary system, rooted in poor theology.

Some of this still goes on but there is no longer a "black Mass." The mourners – or survivors – have to be content with the scriptures of the day and a mention of the deceased in the General Intercessions (the Prayers of the Faithful, a Vatican II innovation). I find it appealing that families gather in a church a year after a death, or every year on the anniversary, or even a month later in what the Irish call "a month's mind," a term which came into the liturgy. They are there, they knew and loved this person, and instead of praying him or her out of purgatory, they simply remember. In recent years I have found this kind of anniversary is one more pastoral opportunity to reach the unchurched. Some family members come to these Masses in a shambling kind of way - they don't want to show disrespect for the dead or upset their mother, etc. No matter, they are there, and it is possible they will respond to a good experience of worship, a prayer that sounds genuine, and a priest who speaks to them afterwards. I tell them that we are remembering with gratitude the gift of this person's life, and trusting that God will unite us.

I kept on with the dialogue Mass in Latin but it strained my ingenuity. It also strained some of my confreres – you have to remember that the whole Liturgical Movement was viewed very dimly by most of the official church. One aspect galled – the laity joining in the prayer of the Mass looked like an infringement on the role of the ordained priest. It even suggested or reminded the heresy hunters of the lay priesthood, the doctrine they associated with Martin Luther, conveniently forgetting that it really began with St. Paul and then St. Peter, and before both apostles, with Jesus Christ. There was considerable suspicion in high places of all this "lay participation stuff." A Jesuit - yes, another one - referred to the magazine *Orate Fratres* which was the principal journal of the Liturgical Movement, and said, "I never pick up that magazine without getting the smell of heresy."

The *Missa Recitatata* (in the required Latin) depended on a group, usually students, who could handle Latin. The principal change I introduced was training a lector to read in English the scriptures that as a priest I was compelled to read in Latin. This ended the slightly absurd practice on Sunday in which the priest, after a Latin whip-through of the gospel, then repeated it in English, and proceeded to give a sermon on anything, but quite often on money, or the sins of the flesh, or missing Mass, or making your Easter duty. The scriptures were rarely the bread that was broken to feed the people. Homily, like liturgy, was an unknown word.

The ultimate breakdown in this attempt to make the Mass intelligible in two languages happened with President Kennedy's funeral in St. Matthew's Cathedral in 1963. Some may recall seeing it on television. Planners of the liturgy had carefully arranged for lectors to give the readings (what we now call the lessons) in English as well as some of the prayers like the sequence, while the priest would say them softly (but rubrically correct) in the official Latin. They reckoned without the celebrant, Boston's Cardinal Richard Cushing, and they should have known it was impossible for him to be soft-spoken. So you had him bawling out Latin while the lector struggled valiantly to make the English heard, even over the microphone. Cushing, of course, was not mean-spirited; he was close to the Kennedys, and his personal words were very genuine.

Parish and University Years

For seven years I was pastor in three small towns of southeast Kansas: Galena, Riverton, and Baxter Springs. I return frequently, and must tell one episode too funny to be true. But it was. If you know anything about haying, it must be done in sunny weather, and all in a few days when the hay is ripened and dry. This was going to happen on my friend's acreage over a long weekend, which necessarily included harvesting on Sunday. I had offered Mass that morning in St. Mary's Church in Joplin, Missouri (just down the road and across the state line). Attending were my hosts, Clarence and Charlene Hill. Clarence was not a Catholic but often came around. Soon after the kind of breakfast one eats when working on a farm, we headed for the fields behind the house. My friends were not really farmers; they ran a large hardware store in town, but to own land and to have cattle was very satisfying. The hay fed the cattle and was sold at the store. And so, to the golden fields. Clarence ran one machine that did the mowing, and he nobly entrusted me with a Rube Goldberg-type apparatus that did the collecting and binding and kicked out the square bales in the wake. All I had to do was aim well. We were clad like the workingmen we were, with big straw hats. The day was blazing. Suddenly my machine stopped running, and Clarence, who could fix anything, was stymied. A friend passing by pulled over and offered his diagnosis, which proved correct. There had been no time to introduce me and the friend began to tease him: "Clarence, if y'd gone to church this mornin' 'stead of workin' on the Lord's Day, this wouldn've happened." Clarence gave a unique answer: "I did go to church and brought the preacher back with me. This here's Father Joe Nolan."

I arrived in this area, which is about as different from Boston as anyone could imagine, in September, 1960. At a farewell luncheon by the Ministerial Alliance seven years later, one of the ministers told me that the clergy in town were convinced that I had been sent there to influence the election. Yes, John Kennedy, Catholic, was running for president. I was astonished. The great majority of my parishioners were Kansas Republicans. The only political connection I ever had was when the whole town jammed our small church for the memorial Mass after Kennedy was assassinated. The ministers also told me that they had elected me treasurer of the Ministerial Alliance the past few years because that was the highest tribute they could give – to be in charge of the money! It was money we used mostly to help transients. In those seven years I had sought out the Protestant clergy and made them my friends. When the beloved Pope John XXIII died, one of them, in tears, broke the news to me as we met outside a grocery store. As time went on I found myself asked to conduct the memorial service at the Elks Lodge, and the weekly "devotional" – a buildup to Christmas – for woodworkers in a small furniture making plant, and then to give the baccalaureate address at high school commencements in each town. The Baptist minister was the first to call me with the news that the students had voted for me. He said, "Considering that there are eighty students in that class and only one Catholic, I'd say that's quite a tribute."

A climate of suspicion and ignorance can indeed change. I was in bible country and not only a Catholic priest but an easterner. The exotic note of having been formerly an FBI agent fascinated them – but perhaps led them to suspect in the beginning that I was undercover for the Democrats. No matter; good things ecumenical continued to happen. The largest undertaker in those towns was Roy Derfelt, a good Baptist; he called one day to ask me to help him purchase a large crucifix to put up in his chapel when he had Catholic funerals. I ordered a handsome one from St. Meinrad Abbey, a robed Christ, suggesting his triumph through the cross. A quarter century later when I flew back to bury a dear old-time parishioner, it was still in use; he had two chapels, one in each town, and carefully carried it to each one as needed.

As for the liturgy in these small parishes, my seven years included Vatican II, which took place from 1962 to 1965. By that time I had begun writing on liturgical subjects, including a column, "World and Worship," in the new *National Catholic Reporter*. All this led to frequent invitations from dioceses everywhere to help explain the changes – or really, what this liturgy business was all about. I limited the number of talks and flew from Joplin (in those days the planes stopped there) to places like New Ulm, Minnesota, Pueblo, Colorado, San Antonio, Los Angeles, and Duluth, Minnesota. The invitation to New Ulm came on the phone; I thought they said New Orleans, and readily agreed.

The invitation to Pueblo came from Bishop Charles Buswell, an eager liturgist and, wonder of wonders, a pastoral bishop. He had been pastor of a large church in Oklahoma City when he was selected by the unusual papal delegate at that time, the Belgian Jean Jadot, who favored candidates with pastoral background. The Duluth invitation came later, when I began to give institutes on preaching as well as liturgy. The bishop there, Paul Anderson, another Jadot success, came from my hometown, Winthrop, Massachusetts. He influenced me towards the priesthood simply by example, by his genuine piety in offering Mass when he returned home. An elderly parishioner said to me, "He spoke Latin so beautifully I could almost understand it." Both of these bishops lived simply, usually with members of their staff, including the laity. They conveyed a very different image of the hierarchical church.

Another welcome trip to Colorado was to the Benedictine abbey at Canyon City, a panel on liturgical change. The heaviest scholar invited was Louis Bouyer of the Oratorian Fathers, whose writings I admired. I was there for the sufficient reason that I was a pastor who was literate in these things, and they always wanted pastoral input. Speaking thus I dared to disagree with Fr. Bouyer who strongly argued that the vernacular should be extended only to the Service of the Word (the scripture readings); for him, the Eucharistic Prayer, then called the Canon, should be kept in universal Latin. I don't remember the arguments but I do remember that he ended them in exasperation, saying "Read my books!"

The most unusual invitation came directly from my own bishop, Mark Carroll, in Wichita. He called me and said, "The Episcopalian liturgists are having their national meeting here and they want you to give the keynote address. You have my permission. I am also going to attend." An invitation I couldn't refuse (and another 400-mile round-trip over the then winding roads from Galena to Wichita). The talk was evidently a success; the applause was prolonged, and perhaps excited by my proposal that the two churches should combine on a joint hymnal. Would that we had. I don't disparage the many efforts to produce our own, but great hymnody was already there. And participation, remember, was still in Latin; our way to participate in vernacular was to sing the usual four hymns.

Another participant was the unusual bishop, James Pike, from San Francisco. He was already a maverick but not yet over the bend (his later opinions were bizarre and his death in Israel was tragic). He insisted that I come to his diocese to speak on liturgy. More permissions needed. The meeting turned out to be at their summer lodge in Santa Rosa. The way there passed through redwood country; I stopped at a Catholic church and found a free-standing altar, just a slab of polished marble resting on the trunk of a redwood tree. The tree was alive and growing when Jesus was born.

This four-star event of the Wichita meeting, I discovered much later, was really the gift of that liturgical giant, Benedictine Father Godfrey Diekmann. He had been the scheduled speaker, and when a conflict arose he advised them that right there in Wichita (well, hardly close by) was a good substitute. Also present was Fr. Gerard Ellard, and in those Kansas years I would visit him at the Jesuit house of studies in St. Mary's, Kansas. One time, arriving on the feast of the Assumption, I expressed surprise at the royal dinner served up, and he told me in his twinkling way that Jesuits could become quite liturgical.

In my small parishes I was on my own, with a more or less permissive bishop (who was also far away). Indeed, Bishop Mark Carroll had flown all the way to Winthrop, Massachusetts from Wichita to ordain me in my home parish. He also told me a few years later that I could read the breviary in English – he did. And the bishop who succeeded him, Leo Byrne, got me into the Council for three weeks in its last year, 1965.

I began liturgical enrichment by putting the children and high school youth into the action. This assures the immediate approval of their parents! Children or families began to bring up the gifts of bread and wine, a practice brand new and not yet official. And of course I explained it; there were even brass tongs to put in individually the altar breads. They were really offering themselves, their life and labor, symbolized by this bread and wine, food and drink. In Advent we shared the honor of lighting the candles week by week - first the oldest parishioner, then the youngest, then the latest married, or the newest parents, and so on. The servers - of all ages - were clad in handsome white albs, girded with a cincture, and wearing a cross on a chain. There were lectors - high school youths willing to prepare the reading, and really to become the master of ceremonies for the Mass. I urged participation, even though it was in Latin. While I read the scripture passages in Latin (to myself, one could say), they proclaimed them in English. The Latin Mass ended with the so-called "last gospel," the sublime prologue of John. For this we printed the best English translation on small cards for the congregation, and everyone read it out loud, together. Before long they knew it by heart, and one day I observed Dennis, four years old, reciting along with the rest. What does a child know? It allowed him to participate, and perhaps seeded his mind with this great passage of Christian belief.

I told the parish that once a month we would set up a temporary altar like a table, and I would offer Mass facing them. This also was anticipatory, but I put it under a catechetical rubric - a good way to learn more of the Mass. The results were electric; the second month the Knights of Columbus Council in Joplin asked if they could come over on a special Sunday to share this "new Mass." On

Holy Thursday, an evening Mass, we surrounded the table altar with low benches and the servers took the place of the apostles. With the help of my best lector, Mike Burke, we read a dialogue account of what the Last Supper was all about. Then Jesus said, "Do this in my memory." We did.

All this "worked," as we say. Here are two clues: Mike and Shawn, high school athletes, put on the white albs for the first time, and one of them said, "Father, are you sure you want us to do this?" "Why not?" "Well, they make us look better than we really are." I told them that was the whole point for all of us – to become what we really are, the followers of Jesus. Beloved of God. The Orthodox would say, to become divine. Forty years later, an email came from a former Mass server, Steve Braun, who had read something I had written about blessed moments when you absolutely know you are in the presence of the Holy - of God. He said, "I remember lining up in the procession Holy Thursday night. We wore crosses, and I caught the light of the candles on my cross. It was only a moment but I knew I was close to God."

We used to kneel a lot but there are only two occasions in Catholic liturgy when prostration is used – the ministers stretched out, face down, on the floor before the altar. One is just before a priest's ordination; he remains prostrate while the Litany of the Saints is being sung. The other is the opening of the Good Friday service. On Good Friday the two principal servers joined me in that ritual. It never needs to be explained.

Children love to participate and I used this approach with Mass servers. Sometimes they were too enthusiastic, as when, at Benediction, David could not reach my shoulders with the humeral veil and simply flung it up from behind. Or Rick, who carried the candle in a procession and accidentally set fire to his hair. He is now a physician in Wichita, and wrote this recently: "I don't know if you realize what an inspiration and wonderful teacher you were to my family and all my friends in the Church while you were in southeast Kansas."

When Rick's father died, Dr. Richard Claiborne, a highly regarded physician in that four-state area, I knew the funeral would exceed the capacity of St. Joseph's Church. Four of my Protestant colleagues offered their churches. The Methodists "won"; it was a new church with a table altar; I just brought in a crucifix and the bread and wine. We also used their hymn book; by that time Catholics were able to sing "*O God Our Help in Ages Past.*"

There were two occasions when our small church was hopelessly crowded with townspeople, and for Masses I planned carefully (this was still the time of Latin and to outsiders our worship appeared mystifying). The first was the death of a parishioner who was a member of a Native American tribe and also of Alcoholics Anonymous. I was not forewarned that both groups always, en masse, attend the leave-taking of their members. The funeral director did alert me that the Native Americans would wish to have their own ritual (after the Catholic one) at the grave site. I assumed he meant some chanted prayers, or even a dance - perfectly okay. "Well," he said, "it's a little more than that - they will want to throw a freshly slaughtered chicken into the grave." No way. He said, "I share your sentiments, but they will do it anyway after you leave."

The other occasion was the death of President Kennedy. The diocese had told us all to have a memorial Mass that Monday. The grief was a tidal wave, and brought the townspeople (mostly Protestant and Republican) crowding into and around the church. How important is ritual and liturgical prayer at this time – I have attended funeral services in other churches which were often grossly sentimental or consisted of endless tributes.

I agree with the observation by Kenneth Woodward (the long-time religious writer in *Newsweek* magazine) that Catholic parishes have missed many opportunities to involve their youth, and should imitate the Mormons, who assign them many functions of service and worship as they grow up. They give them titles and responsibilities, and also a sense of importance, of being needed. We could do much more, with the awarding of acolyte, chorister, lector, porter (the care of sacred things), eucharistic minister, catechist, and - this especially - participation in outreach programs to the needy. To the nearby nursing homes, retirement centers, or to people who simply need visiting and conversation. If there is not a service dimension to church we are not faithful to the gospel.

The vestments for Mass were handsome. I kept one chasuble in the old style (irreverently called fiddle back) because it was so richly embroidered with the cross and symbols of the Passion; we used it only on Good Friday. And on that day we used visual symbols: the nails (railroad spikes) and a crown of thorns were brought on pillows in the silent procession, and placed by the cross. On occasion we brought the outside inside, filling much of the sanctuary with the fall foliage, or the abundance of dogwood blossoms for Holy Thursday. Although Thanksgiving began as a religious holiday in the east it was in the midwest that I found the Catholics expected a religious service - Protestants did it! So we had Mass, and prepared a horn of plenty, fruits and vegetables tumbling over, and a procession at the Offertory of things to be thankful for - everything from a new baby, a recent marriage, a recovery from illness, the Declaration of Independence (a facsimile copy), and fun in sports - the high school athletes were persuaded to bring up their winning basketball. The key to all this, of course, was participation - and to look upon every day, all life, as a blessing and an offering.

Looking back, I wish we had had more "outreach" from the two parishes – commitment to good works. But helping a neighbor was (and still is) taken for granted in midwestern communities. They were indeed good years. I had barely moved into the parish when the Sisters of Mercy called from nearby Joplin, Missouri, and said, "We read about your appointment in the paper, and saw that you had two degrees in history. God has sent you, because we need a history teacher for our high school." Sisters can very persuasive, so I taught there for all seven years, swapping for their religious instruction of our children. I shifted to religion after the first year. That meant I could prepare more lectors to participate in the youth Masses.

Even though the Council was unfolding and changing minds, this was still a time of conformity, and I was somewhat surprised that I "got away with stuff." Many years later I learned one reason why. Bishop Byrne told Father Leonard (he of the original dialogue Mass) that he had received a letter from a visitor to the parish who praised the way I conducted funerals. I tried to think back. One of the major families were Lebanese in origin, named Joseph. They were happily part of everything. When Jappour, the beloved father, died, I had the wake service in the church with the body present, and the prayers included six psalms along with scripture readings from a booklet I had prepared. I don't recall more, but the tradition of "great funerals" has continued, always with sermons on the resurrection and a eulogy (long before it became official) by a family member. Eulogies at that time were allowed only for priests, a typical clerical approach, and it seemed wrong to me not to have someone speak in thanksgiving for a person's life.

Sheila Cavanaugh, a well-known motivational speaker, tells people that we should write letters of praise, not just complaints. Someone who did that for me was partially responsible for my "liturgical parishes." It was not a golden age; it was just that good things happened.

Remember, in those early days to really participate in the Mass was something new and exciting for Catholics. On a trip through Glacier National Park with a seminarian and four high school students, we offered the Assumption Day Mass in a lodge far up the mountain. This was my crowd - I suppose you could say disciples - and they ringed the altar, sharing the Latin responses. All this delighted the overnight visitors in the lodge. Those were days when you did not omit, even on vacation, a holyday Mass. And to actually "pray the Mass" was like unwrapping a long-hidden treasure.

In 1971 I was asked to come to New Orleans to give a brief course in sacramental theology. What I remember, besides the joy of eating in that city, was the distinct difference among the seminarians who, in those bygone days, numbered about twenty-eight in the deacon class. About twenty of these were casually attired; the others swept in with full cassock and collar. That split indicated an attitude towards change which has continued, except that seminarians now, much fewer in number, are mostly inclined to be conservative, to emerge as very formal, rubrically-minded priests, conscious of their dignity.

The other memorable incident in New Orleans was joining a congregation, mostly black, with a fellow liturgist for Sunday Mass. He tried to prepare me; he said, "They really sing!" And so they did; the huge robed choir led the people in the kind of robust song you just don't get in most Catholic churches. It could be a sense of rhythm and moving with the body; in this church the choir danced or slithered up the aisle three times: once for the opening procession; again, to bring up the offerings; and a third, to begin communion. (The late Clarence Rivers, a great black liturgist, once said to me at Grailville in Ohio, "You white folks just don't have it!")

In 1967 I received permission to pursue graduate studies at Harvard (on my own limited income); it had been flattering to be "the pastor who could speak from experience" on the liturgical circuit, but I felt the need to go deeper into theology. Those years were full of social turmoil - the Vietnam War and in 1968, the murders of Martin Luther King and Robert Kennedy - and that affected campus liturgies and much more. The Masses for students at Harvard were orchestrated by a resourceful chaplain, Richard Griffin, then a Jesuit, who was good at balancing many views. He dared to risk offering a lay preacher at one big Sunday Mass; she was Bernadette Brooten, scripture scholar in the making, who gave a homily on the Song of Songs, the first reading of that day, and affirmed very much that it was God's endorsement of sexual love, not just some metaphor for the way God loved the church. I began to offer a weekday Mass for students who gathered around the table in Phillips House, and also for the Thomas More Society, Catholic students at Harvard Law School. I still offer small group or family Masses on special occasions; it all began around a table, and the second Mass, if you like to think that way, was at the inn in Emmaus when "they knew him in the breaking of the bread."

Bishop Helder Camara, the apostle of the poor in Recife, Brazil, visited Harvard and I concelebrated with him at the student center, preparing a special liturgy. Then came a request from the Divinity School to arrange and conduct an ecumenical service for Good Friday. A student working with me said, "We must have Tenebrae." Well, yes - an abbreviated form (and in the daylight). Tenebrae had been the three-night service in Holy Week when the Lamentations were sung in plaintive melodies, both Latin and Hebrew, as the candles one by one were extinguished, leaving the church in darkness. We dug up a Tenebrae candleholder and extinguished the candles as the Passion account was read. There were a few carefully crafted prayers in the service, and an interval of silence but not the fifteen minutes that the Quaker participant wished! And the singing of the Negro spiritual, *Were You There when They Crucified My Lord?* The soloist was a large black woman who worked in the student dining halls, and who sang in a heart-rending mode. The learned professors and seekers of degrees were all silenced by her. I wanted a symbol of brokenness on the center table as the people gathered for the hour – a beautiful ceramic cup already shattered in pieces. My student aide said this was too expensive an idea, but my solution was to find a kiln and ask for a flawed one, a discard. He wanted to break the cup when the narrator reached the death of Jesus but that would have been too obvious. The broken pieces were there from the beginning.

There was one surprise. On the back of the single sheet program I had put in my best chancery script Sydney Carter's version of *The Lord of the Dance*, the old Shaker hymn. It expresses the whole life, and new life, of Jesus the Christ, and is well known. The unexpected happened as we arose to leave. A black student who was a superb dancer suddenly grabbed the soloist and they whirled around the open space in the church, singing

The Lord of the Dance. Real liturgy indeed has surprise elements like these that lift the heart.

I learned more of liturgy, or really the symbolic language of religion, from an extraordinary professor, Raimundo Panikkar. The course was *Worship and Secular Man,* which resulted in a text by that name that I later used when invited to teach at Boston College. It is a provocative, probing work, and possibly the easiest of his dense writings. Panikkar is a world scholar; I am not but we had a common interest in tennis as well as symbol! He helped me to understand world religions, and later on, when he taught at the University of California at Santa Barbara and I was a "writer in residence" at Franciscan Communications in Los Angeles, we often met and each offered Mass at Santa Barbara's famed mission church. I had first met him in the summer of 1967 when we were both teaching summer courses at Manhattanville College, near New York City. What he has offered me all these years is of the greatest value, the gift of friendship.

Another advantage of being at Harvard in those years was to see the progress of the St. Paul Boys Choir. It was located in the parochial school of the nearby St. Paul's Church, a Romanesque structure where liturgy and preaching were considered important. It was here that Theodore Marier began in 1963 to implement his dream of a boys' choir school. I knew him well because we were two of those unusual lay people in the 1940s who were interested in the liturgical movement. Indeed we were rebels *with* a cause. The Mariers had three growing children, and Ted and Alice asked me to prepare the twin boys, then twelve, as acolytes, Mass servers. That training was done in parochial schools and they were enrolled in a public school in Belmont. I took them in hand, and their first Mass was celebrated with great style in Boston College's lovely gothic chapel, St. Mary's. In 1949 Ted had recruited me for the men's scholar (Bernard Law, then a Harvard student, was also a singer). And

Ted gave all of us lessons in Gregorian chant, with all the nuances of performance that a good conductor demands.

As for the boys choir, Ted told me often that it was past time to emulate the great choir schools of Europe, notably in England. Anyone who has gone to the cathedrals there, or to Oxford and Cambridge for Evensong, would agree. Had we no goals for a Catholic culture in Boston that would reclaim the great music tradition of the church that had nurtured Gregorian chant and produced polyphony and Palestrina? A choir school is a costly proposition because ideally it is all scholarship, and must cover academic subjects for the young boys until the time their voices changed. There was no way students could live in, and they came stoically every day from all over, singing the daily Mass in St. Paul's and preparing for Sunday. They often sang for their supper - weddings on Saturday, traveling to the churches in an old school bus with Ted Marier quite often the driver. His lovable wife Alice was always present, a mother to the boys, and John Dunne was the organist (he succeeded as director upon Marier's death). Now they turn the church into a wonderful concert hall several times a year. But the liturgy still is the most important function, and the group, now known as the Boston Boys' Choir, is an esteemed part of the cultural scene.

Few people succeed with their dream and leave a legacy as Marier did; his love of music and skills in Gregorian chant made him a teacher at Catholic University and Manhattanville, and a revered figure everywhere. He began playing piano early, and told me that his first job – a child who could not even reach the pedals on the piano – was to play the music for the silent films in the local theatre. Another anecdote from the 1950's is priceless. Senator John Kennedy was to marry Jacqueline Bouvier in a Rhode Island parish, and Cardinal Cushing of Boston was to be the celebrant. He asked Ted to play the organ and plan the music. Ted went down to look over the scene, and discovered the organ was in such disrepair that the pedals did not even work. When he complained to the pastor, the latter said, "But the keyboard works, and Mrs. O'Brien plays lovely hymns on it all the time!" "Then let Mrs. O'Brien play for the wedding!" retorted Ted. What this meant, I told him, was that he had refused to play for the wedding of a future president. No matter.

The other incident involved Cushing when he was first named an auxiliary bishop. He was confronted with singing the Holy Week liturgy, largely in chant, and called Ted to come over and coach him. Ted began with his usual vigor and thoroughness, cautioning to descend on the tops of the notes to avoid flatting, and using a few technical terms like "quilisma." At this point Cushing broke in and said, "Ted, cut out the theories and just give me the tunes!"

The liturgy was changing everywhere and experiments were common. On a Boston street I ran into Father Joe Appleyard who asked me to take one of the student Masses at Boston College, where participation was vigorous and, of course, accompanied by new music and guitars. At the same time I was asked to take a Sunday Mass on the campus of Sacred Heart College at midnight; the request came from Sister Elizabeth White (then Mother White; the Sacred Heart nuns were changing, too). She was (and still is) one of those highly educated and gifted nuns, her fields both English and music. Why midnight? Although things were changing these were still the days of parietals - administrators in place of parents - and the students were required to attend Mass on Sunday. They also had to be back on campus Saturday night (really Sunday morning) at 1:00 a.m. If they could only make this midnight tryst with God, they could then sleep blissfully through Sunday morning. The Mass was totally crowded.

The Jesuits at Holy Cross in Worcester were next in those days of exciting "new Masses." Student Masses there on Sunday nights in the ornate marble church were also crowded, and had extraordinary participation. The singing was led by a gifted Jesuit composer, and the most striking feature was the surge of the students into the sanctuary, as many as possible, where they offered the altar breads that would become their communion. They remained there for the eucharistic prayer (would that it could have been sung with them). The Lenten Masses at Holy Cross featured a "Great Preachers Series." Remarkable in itself, considering how little attention Catholics had given to preaching. And also quite flattering to be included. I asked who had preceded me and learned, with some dismay, that the previous two weeks had featured Daniel Berrigan, already a Jesuit hero, and the Dean of Harvard Divinity School, Krister Stendahl, the esteemed scripture scholar. One aspect about preaching was becoming evident to me: if you did it well - a decent or compelling homily on Sunday - people sought you out in gratitude! I have made many and lasting friendships thus. From 1984 on I have preached regularly at St. Ignatius Church, adjoining Boston College, and for many summers in Osterville, "down the Cape." There I offered two series, one on "Eternal Life," the other, "Belief in God." They can still be classed as homilies - the Sunday scriptures are easily "fitted in" - and I felt strongly about the need to build a resurrection faith. Preaching, and offering Mass, have long been the compelling and exalting aspects of my life.

The Return to the Vernacular

That was the title of a pamphlet I wrote in 1958, arguing strongly that it was time to change the language of the liturgy. I reached that position slowly; in fact, I can remember insisting on the case for Latin with a naval classmate in the bunk below me (it was indoctrination school for new officers). He gave some of the practical reasons for English that I would later adopt, and ignored my rash statement that the church would never change (how often we hear that remark still, from people with no sense of history).

I liked Latin, and studied it through high school and college, but my first acquaintance came as a Mass server. At the age of eleven in my hometown parish you were admitted to the ranks of the acolytes, but only after a massive mental effort to learn all the Latin responses of the Mass - a lot of them - and give them by heart at appropriate times. And totally without comprehension. But never mind; to be a Mass server was worth the pain. We wore the usual cassock and surplice but more colorful vestments were on hand for cross-bearers and thurifers and special occasions like carrying the torches to flank the Blessed Sacrament in procession. The mystery of incense – or rather, the making of clouds of incense – never seemed to be mastered by most Catholic servers. In later years I learned to marvel at the Orthodox liturgy where thuribles are swung like whips and fragrant clouds drift in the air

No one thought it strange that we did not have to learn the English equivalent of what we parroted at Mass, usually at top speed. Too bad, because the Latin rite for Mass opened with a psalm (Psalm 42) dialogued between priest and server; it began, "I will go unto the altar of God." And the response, "To God who gives joy to my youth." (It still comes back: "Introibo ad altare Dei, ad Deum qui laetificat juventutem meum.") To walk or bike the long distance to church for an entire week in the early morning was something we did not complain about. We served. We were, in our own way, important. The Mass was not supposed to take place without one of us present (we didn't know it, but we represented the church). We actually prayed in the ritual for God to forgive the priest's sins! And those lofty eminences took notice of us. One of them rewarded my search to know more about Catholicism by giving me a copy of Fr. Conway's *Question Box*; copies are surely kept in libraries today, along with much other literature, as an example of how we, or the church, thought in those days. All problems were solved. There were no doubts, and no one else was quite right.

But back to Latin: in my college years I did know what I was saying at Mass, and perhaps even praying, and my experience as a layman with a dialogue Mass in Latin and then in the early years of parish ministry was satisfying. Why couldn't it be that way for everyone else? The St. Andrew's Missal had parallel columns of Latin and English. And certainly the use of this mother language, classical and ecclesial for so many centuries, united us all, a world church. I am sure that I argued those points in print and in person. But at some point I came to realize that Latin really divided most of the Catholic world from understanding, from lending our minds as well as our hearts and will to prayer. A turning point came with a letter published somewhere from a priest in India. He said angrily, "You talk about lay missals as the solution. How little you people know! My Catholics here in India for the most part cannot read. And if they could, they could not afford to buy a book."

I made a similar point in my pamphlet: "Ask the Glenmary Fathers if their backwoods converts are going to be at ease with 'the simple Latin phrases.' Ask your own friends and family what '*O salutaris*' means." And Keith Pecklers' book, *Dynamic Equivalence,* quotes this letter from a sister who is answering the defense of Latin by the eminent scholar Christopher Dawson:

> They (if they come to church at all) are dead tired from the daily struggle to make a livelihood; the pace of our times is most demanding, harassing. When the working people come to church, they are not ready for complicated mental exercises. Moreover, a quick hurried leafing through an English-Latin has come from a Protestant theologian, Ronald Goetz book, trying to keep up with a priest, does not fill their innermost needs. How often in my long years of labor among the 'border-line Catholics' have I not met people who, with every bit of good will, have attended our services and then have turned away in discouragement saying, 'I don't know what's going on.'... If I go to a Protestant church, there I gain something, even if much is missing of what I like in the Catholic Church.

The book just cited, *Dynamic Equivalence,* is a must-read for anyone interested in the heroic labor of so many to bring about the final return to the vernacular language accomplished at Vatican II and by two popes, Pius XII and Paul VI. The group of scholars and linguists known as ICEL (International Commission on English in the Liturgy), appointed by the bishops' conferences in English-speaking countries, has labored many years to produce the English version now in use, and an improved version now on the shelf because ICEL appears to be sidelined (or silenced) by Rome. The dispute has been long and sharp over the norm to use in translation. A "dynamic equivalence" seeks to render the meaning in current language; others argue for a more literal translation to safeguard doctrine.

An example of the difficulty in translation is the single phrase in Latin, "Credo in unum Deum." It certainly looks like "I believe," not "We believe," and a correspondent in *The Tablet* argued bitingly that the present translation is "unverifiable and at its worst, untrue." But that called forth a rebuttal from a layman who said that the text of the first seven general councils of the church all used the plural verb in Greek and in Latin. He further notes that the Creed of Pope Paul VI, which enlarges the Nicene Creed, uses "we believe" (*credimus*) about eighteen times. In an American dispute on the same issue, a well-known liturgist said that "I believe" is proper for the Apostles Creed when it is used at the baptism of a new Christian, but thereafter "We believe" is fitting for the assembly because they affirm their faith as a community and support each other in that faith together.

Peckler's book is researched with a scholar's care and is fascinating reading. There is much more to the history of vernacular than most of us knew. For instance, Saints Cyril and Methodius fought strongly to have the liturgy expressed in Slavonic. And this was in the ninth century. After the American Revolution, Archbishop John Carroll argued in vain for the use of English in worship, pointing to rites within the church with small membership but who were allowed their own liturgical language while the English speaking countries were forced to do without.

This effort to persuade the official church to worship as they did in the beginning - in the language of the people - was fittingly carried on by lay people as well as priests and scholars. The Vernacular Society in England soon had an American counterpart which published a vigorous journal called *Amen.* The title came from St. Paul, who said, "How can one who holds the place of the layman say the 'Amen' to your thanksgiving since he does not know what you are saying?" (*1 Cor 14:16*). (One would think that text alone would carry the day.)

There are people who think Jesus spoke Latin, and the Mass was always in Latin. There was even a group in the 8th century called the "trilinguists," who insisted the Mass should be celebrated only in the three languages affixed to the cross: Latin, Greek, and Hebrew. After Pope John XXIII, in a short-lived and uncharacteristic move, published the encyclical, *Veterum Sapientiae,* endorsing Latin, for a priest to be associated with the Vernacular Society often meant suspicion or censure. When I was asked to become president of the society I promptly ducked, to avoid silencing. The Liturgical Conference could not get the slightest concession from Rome to use the vernacular in the Service of the Word at its annual meeting, and was constrained to declare officially that they were separate from the Vernacular Society. Henceforth we met separately - like a revolutionary cadre!

The title of Pope John's encyclical means "the wisdom of the ancients" and the best reply to its arguments came from priests in the Orient who said, "They are not *our* ancients." And indeed, thanks to the theology of Karl Rahner and the surprising appointments by Pope Paul VI of cardinals from around the world, we in the west slowly realized that we are, or should be, a world church.

Part of the opposition to any new movement comes from the large group who don't like change. It was Cardinal Newman who said, "In another life it will not be so, but to live here and now means to change. And to be perfect is to change often." The most basic paradigm (working model) in the church is one of change: from death to life. Those who resist change are usually called conservative. But true liturgical reforms aim to conserve or regain the original power that the first followers of Jesus felt profoundly, and which led them to change themselves and much of their known world. The opposition to the vernacular reminds me of the upset for some, including priests, when Rome proposed to allow evening Masses, including a Saturday vigil that would "count" for Sunday. The only exception to the morning hour for so long a time had been the midnight Mass at Christmas, of course, but also, by indult, midnight Masses at special shrines like those of the Blessed Sacrament. In college years that provided a cheap date (and late night) for some of us. Our parents could hardly object if we were going to Mass! And the only expense was coffee and doughnuts afterwards. I recall a group of priests objecting to this new innovation - Mass in the evening - because "it had never been done before." The argument ended when someone dryly remarked, "For God's sake, it was the Last Supper, not the Last Breakfast!"

A recent statement from Rome on language and the liturgy urges a new emphasis on learning enough Latin to facilitate celebrating together on world wide occasions. I agree, although English is now the lingua franca. Learn both, and remember, in all this discussion, how Jewish children toil over Hebrew, and Muslim youngsters learn Arabic. Learning Latin in school is gaining somewhat. As one student told me, "I took it in high school in order to learn English well." Of course – but we have shrunk our curricula in so many ways to math, technology, and science that we are lucky even to retain English (indeed we have not, if one is thinking of common skills in writing a good sentence).

Isn't the vernacular question settled? No. We have it – in fact, the church in any big city now offers Mass in multiple languages. There has been a strong vocal minority who still want the Mass in Latin. The church allows it with the new rite, and Pope John Paul II, against a majority world-wide opinion of bishops, allowed some use of the "old Mass," the missal that was approved by Pius VI after the Council of Trent. In July of 2007 his successor, Benedict XVI, broadened this permission, stating that henceforth there would be two ways to celebrate the Mass, the ordinary way "as is," and the extraordinary way, the Tridentine rite. This arrangement was opposed by many, including bishops in France and Germany, and the pope presciently called for an assessment in three years of how well this dual arrangement works out. Recently a priest properly credentialed turned up in that part of Massachusetts known as Cape Cod, looking to buy a house where he could construct a chapel to have "the Mass as it used to be." "Ad Deum qui laetificat juventutem meum." I love that psalm but I won't be going to Father Oldschool's Mass. My focus now on language in the liturgy is to urge and offer prayers that are far more expressive and scriptural than the present texts.

The argument is still made that wherever one traveled in earlier days one could feel at home with the Mass in Latin. I too have traveled everywhere and can identify with the action of the Mass, if not the actual words in another language. But there are two reasons against the "Latin everywhere makes you feel at home" argument. First, the majority of people are *not* traveling most of the time. Or at all. And the vernacular reform, like so many new-old practices, is a classic case of losing some values and gaining others which have been judged more needed. No major transition is accomplished without considerable pain, a feeling of loss which is more than nostalgia. But there is a strong argument for the greater good. The world traveler matches his discomfort in losing Latin against the Pentecostal splendor which is now true: "Each has heard in his own language the wonderful works of God" (*Acts 2.11*).

Preface to Section 2

The narrative thus far has been autobiographical because my understanding of liturgy is life-centered - my own, and others. What follows is doctrinal, liturgical theology, but still seen through the prism of experience. We live in a time when, it has been well said, we do not answer so much to the experience of authority as to the authority of experience. So, why do people go to Mass? What is their experience? Is it gladdening, a reaffirming of their Catholic faith? Is reciting a creed (and always the same creed) really helpful to inform and sustain belief? Or is it a necessary reference point that came from the Councils and the teaching church? Who meditates on the creed or the other prayers of Mass? Does the awareness of the Real Presence and participation in the official prayer deepen an interior life?

As to why people come, the older answer was often based on obedience to church law, and fear if disobedient. The newer answer is still forthcoming. Our worship is no longer the phenomenon of the past when large churches were filled at multiple Masses. The decline has happened for various reasons, such as disaffection with the church, and more lately, the lack of priests. So why do people go? To pray, and many to join others in prayer. To meet other people. The Mass can be a place where community is expressed or emerges. They go to be in the Real Presence, so I discuss what that means. And to join themselves to Christ's offering, although this is not yet fully established or understood.

The Mass is centered on the Real Presence, but in us as well as the host. Flesh as well as bread. It is also a proclamation of the scriptures, but there is the danger of simply taking what the bible says without the aid of biblical scholarship. The Mass is a place to encounter the Real Presence in the people and in the word proclaimed and received, and this is a new emphasis. It is a time for reverence; this is old but still important. It is a time for the sacrament of Holy Communion, and for most older people this is new. What should one think about the recent suggestion by a Roman cardinal that at huge outdoor Masses (such as the funeral of John Paul II) communion should not be given, for reasons of respect and logistics?

Does the renewal of vows at Easter really become meaningful? Or offering the bread and wine reflect a self-offering? Can we use the arts of celebrating and song within boundaries of rubrics and common sense? Are some aspects of the liturgy (think of sacramentals) close to magic for some?

Other reasons to "go to Mass": because it is something spiritual, a good thing to do. And for some, the most important thing they do. The Mass - indeed, all worship - is a symbolic act; consider how symbols work. They are multivalent - thus the Real Presence is in both the consecrated host and the people. Symbols are participatory. Yes, at Mass we are invited to praise and give thanks, a loving response to God's gift. Symbols are integrative. Here, in this place, and by this action, I become more myself, more "in Christ," the Living One who is the center of my faith. Symbols are fitting. And the food and drink we use, the bread and wine, come from the earth, the primary gift of the Creator, and "the work of our own hands." Symbols are integrative. Participation helps me to be whole, on the way to holiness. Prayer anywhere, but especially the prayer of Mass, always seeks a communion with God in Christ.

UNDERSTANDING THE LITURGY

The Nature of Worship (Kierkegaarde)

The Danish theologian and critic of the Christian church, Soren Kierkegaard, offers a schema, apparently very simple, to help us understand liturgy, or Christian worship. He says that it unfolds like a drama or play, and in every play there are three essential components. They are the actors, the audience, and the prompter - the person in the wings who corrects mistakes, supplies the right lines if needed, helps to keep the drama going. Now who takes which role in Christian worship? It seems obvious that the actors are the clergy. They have the leading roles, and in liturgical churches they dress for the occasion. The audience, of course, is the congregation. Who is the prompter in the worship scene? Obviously the Holy Spirit, providing us with nothing less than the sacred text, the word of God, inspiring us in giving the sermon, and so on.

Is that it? No, Kierkegaard says that's all wrong. If we think this is the way liturgy proceeds, no wonder it isn't working very well and gaining positive results. And if our worship is a model for life itself, no wonder the results are stingy, meager. So let's reassemble the cast.

First, the clergy are not the ones on the stage putting on this play. It used to look that way, but now the whole congregation is in on this action. All of us together are the body of Christ, seeking the will and doing the work of the Father. Liturgy is a paradigm or model for Christian life, and in the drama of human existence, both comic and tragic, we each take different roles and use our various gifts to bring about the kingdom. In neither liturgy nor life are we meant to be a passive audience, waiting to be entertained or told what to do.

So we are *all* on stage. Who, then, is the prompter? This *is* the special role of the priest. Of the deacon. Of the lector. Of those who prepare the liturgy, the celebration. They give us the text, which is the word of God, and sometimes help us in the interpretation.

And where is God? God is the audience, taking in all this, observing how well we fulfill the assignments given to us. Are we forgiving, as Christ forgives – and commands? Are we loving? Just? Sharing – and seeking out especially the poor, the marginalized, as Jesus did so often. Are we serving those who need us, faithful to the One who said, "I am among you as one who serves." Assignments began with our baptism and have continued ever since – through every sacrament, sermon and gospel, and patient instruction by so many.

The "Old Mass" (of Paul V, post-Trent)

A review of the "old Mass," as celebrated before 1970 and the reform of Pope Paul VI, will give us perspective. The Latin Mass began with a psalm at the foot of the altar, dialogued between the priest and one or two servers. They followed it with a long – really long – confession of sins, prayed speedily. Rubrics for this were carefully, even vigorously observed by the servers – kneeling, bowed down, turning twice to the priest - "Et tibi, Pater" when the servers began their confession, and finally "Et te, Pater," when they actually prayed that God might forgive the priest. A neat exchange of roles. The most vigorous response came with striking the breast three times while confessing "mea culpa, mea culpa, mea maxima culpa." The priest then ascended the steps, praying silently, kissed the altar, moved to the right (called the Epistle side), and read an entrance verse (Introit). Then to the middle for the Kyrie, sometimes the Gloria, and a prayer. All this was facing the wall or the tabernacle, not the people. An epistle was read, never translated, mostly from St. Paul. The celebrant would turn several times in the Mass to say "Dominus vobiscum." ("The Lord be with you"). And the server would answer, "Et cum spiritu tuo." The old translation was

"And with your spirit." After the epistle the server transferred the big heavy book to the left, the Gospel side; this was quite a feat for smaller boys because it involved a genuflection while balancing the book. He was also charged with ringing a hand bell no less than eight times during the Mass. The Italian film so many have enjoyed, *Cinema Paradiso,* has a hilarious scene where the small boy server falls asleep *before* and *between* the two consecrations and thus misses both ringing of the bells.

The priest then read the gospel in Latin and if it was Sunday, moved to the pulpit, repeated the gospel in English and preached the sermon. This could be what dictionaries describe as "a moralistic discourse." The subject frequently followed a syllabus; creed, code, and cult was a favorite choice of chanceries. One would preach for a series of Sundays on the articles of the creed, then on the Ten Commandments and the six commandments of the church, and finally on the Mass and the sacraments. The gospel selections were the same every year and favored Matthew's gospel which emphasizes the church as institution.

It now seems incredible that so much of the scriptures was left out, but this ended the Mass of instruction or catechumens. It was further devalued by a church law that to miss this part of Mass was only a venial sin. So you had to get there before the offertory prayers to stay in the state of grace. In no sense were we a people formed by the word. In fact, older Catholics will tell you that they were forbidden, or at least discouraged from reading the bible. And indeed it can lead one astray, as Peter's epistle warns. But imagine not hearing the great parables from Luke, the promises of eternal life in John, the scenes of Jesus at prayer in Mark. And never hearing the great words from the Hebrew prophets: Amos, calling for justice; Micah, with the now beloved passage about justice and peace and walking in humility before the Lord; and the later prophets telling of God's everlasting love.

After the Creed the Mass was divided into Offertory, Consecration, and Communion. There were no Offertory processions or Prayers of the Faithful. And for most people, no receiving of communion except at Christmas and Easter. Pious societies sometimes received monthly. Fasting to receive was imposed from midnight on. (In daylight saving time we would, with superb casuistry, push the legal limit to one o'clock, real time.) The fast included water, and led to scruples by some over accidentally swallowing toothpaste or, God help us, even a few drops of rain. The Sanctus began the Canon, now called the Eucharistic Prayer. The Consecration and the Elevation were the most solemn moments, signaled by the bell and sometimes by incense. This was (and still is) a moment of deep devotion, an awareness that God had come among us. There was no emphasis on the final prayer of the Canon, no sense of gathering together both people and priest into the one Christ, one great offering of our lives to the Father.

Priestly etiquette or rubrics was extensive: the way hands were held, genuflections performed, fingers that touched the sacred host kept apart. Different levels of voice were required, a low tone for the canon, suggesting its mystery. (I got in early trouble by ignoring this; I felt that people should at least hear the Latin.) All sacred vessels were rinsed and scoured after communion, and only by the priest. All these rubrics were to emphasize the sacredness of what was happening, and especially the sublime act of changing the bread and wine into the body and blood of Christ. We were often reminded that the priest, sacramentally and in a very real way, brought Christ down from heaven. It was a major and, to some, a shocking statement by the church to declare officially in Vatican II that Christ was already present in the word and in the people. The priest's role was not so much to "bring him down" as to alert us to his presence and unite us and form us as members of his body.

It was indeed possible to love this Mass – it was the only one we knew. No one then dreamed that one day the Mass would have lay readers of scripture, men and women who also assisted with communion, or processions out so that the priest, who formerly vanished into the sacristy, could then greet the people. Nor did we expect the custom of the Pax to be extended - the people greeting each other with the sign of peace. That was a strictly clerical rite, done only at a solemn high Mass (what some liked to call "a three priest Mass." For example, "Mother had a three-priest funeral.")

The solemn high Mass involved a deacon and a sub-deacon (who were usually ordained priests), and many of the prayers were sung. The deacon would read the gospel (but not necessarily preach). The sub-deacon was just part of the line-up; the three officiants moved and bowed in concert on the steps of the altar. It was a choreographed performance, painstakingly learned. A high Mass involved only one priest but still the prayers were sung. These Masses presented an aesthetic problem because priests received little or no training in singing, and the preface of the Mass, his main challenge, could be sung completely off key. It was simply awful. It has been a huge gain for everyone to deliver tone deaf and musically illiterate priests from this requirement!

It is really dismaying to think what was *not* part of a seminary curriculum, preparing priests to offer worship. Rubrics, yes, but not really presiding – and leading. There was little or no training in singing or the place of music in the liturgy. Or in preaching – the standard homiletics course was hugely inadequate. And biblical scholarship is taking a long time to overcome a Catholic fundamentalism.

This description of the Tridentine Mass was in the past tense. But it is now present, following the official permission (Motu Proprio) of Benedict XVI. The same limiting features are there.

The Mass Today

There is great continuity in Catholic worship; the Mass is offered everywhere, all the time. Of course, it is the life of the church. It can have the great and moving solemnity that the whole world shared with the funeral of Pope John Paul II, or it can have the full-throated enthusiasm of university or high school students with their own music, and very much involved. Or the enthusiastic presence of children answering their own official eucharistic prayer, acting out the gospels, delighting us with their insights, guided by great catechists. Recently in a friend's parish, when sending out the children for their own Service of the Word, I called them up first for a blessing and one small boy leaped into my arms. More than once I have ended Mass (the recessional) by taking children with me, or an infant in my arms. All this is not "cute"; it is the most vital sign I know of new life, life as a gift to be taken gratefully and used well. And this is the heart of all that we do.

Worshippers often meet in a new setting – churches built or remodeled after the reform have avoided the long oblong nave which put people so far away. We are familiar with an arrangement that is two thirds of a circle, even with large churches, and to celebrate Mass in such a church is a notably different experience. This style is not an absolute; the cathedral in San Francisco and the new one in Los Angeles are compelling in their design, and a worthy art adorns them. What a challenge to build a church! Although the Mass can be offered everywhere, we need great churches, and good art in each of them.

There is a serious conflict of opinion as to the success of the reform that began with Vatican II and became definitive in 1969 with the *Novus Ordo* of Pope Paul VI. There are organizations who not only favor the Latin but protest strongly and learnedly at what they consider the loss of the sacred, the sense of mystery, perhaps even of transcendence. The present pope expressed (before his election) his own thoughts about the loss of beauty. I find this especially true in too many American churches.

Has the holy, the numinous, the awe one should feel at times before God – and in worship - has this really been lost? Some of the external changes included the loss of genuflection (for a proper reason; in most churches the reserved and consecrated hosts are no longer in a tabernacle above or behind the altar, but at a special altar to one side). We have not succeeded, and should, with a bow to the altar and cross as a reverential gesture when entering the church or the pew. And now there is a ritual for receiving communion, a small bow, which is often difficult to coordinate with the procession and the act of receiving the host. And, of course, silence has vanished; we talk in church. We even greet people as they arrive, and in some churches are invited to greet each other before the Mass begins.

In weighing all this, one conclusion is that you can't have everything, at least in a single Mass. The warmth and cordiality of many parishes with these new practices is a gain. So is the sign of peace, even if it sometimes gets too demonstrative. For one small girl it is the highlight; she asks her parents, "When do we get to the pleased-t'meetcha part"? This is some contrast to a Mass in Michigan in 1970 when the custom was new. It was Christmas Eve and the night the astronauts went around the moon (reciting Genesis 1 as they orbited). I offered the sign of peace to an eager little girl on the end of the pew and her father struck her hand away.

Many features of "the new Mass" are a great gain, such as the lay ministers that assist it. The processions, the greeting of people from the once silent and disappearing pastor, the return of almost the whole assembly to communion, the sense that to participate in Mass itself brings about the forgiveness of sins. There is even a slow improvement in preaching. Who does not see all this as gain?

If all this is people-centered (one of the criticisms made) we should remember that this is the original definition of liturgy: a work of the people. And much of what they do around the altar is, as we have noted, an expression of their baptismal dignity, more particularly of their share in the priesthood of Christ. It is sound doctrine that we have only one priest - Jesus Christ.

There is a tension between two approaches, two values. One is adoration, the other is oblation (or offering). If the right understanding of Mass is, as it should be, an oblation, an offering of the whole Christ, a commission to love and serve the Lord by contributing each in one's own way to the coming of the kingdom - does all this necessarily conflict with adoration, silence, prayer, inner consecration? No, and there must always be an *internal* participation and times for silence, a really deep silence. And an attitude by the priest that is not cheery or casual but genuinely and consistently prayerful. No more "Good morning, everyone" (warmth and cordiality at the end, yes). And the music must reach those moments of exaltation that only music and great art (like the church building itself) can give.

It is easy to feel a bond of affection with the people at Mass, and not just the children. They are so varied, each reflecting the mystery of life and the future. They can be bearing the weight of so many problems. And this presents a challenge to the liturgist and especially the preacher. A Marist father and close friend, Albert Di Ianni, tells me of his father's advice to him when he was newly ordained. He said, "Life is hard – a lot harder then you will ever know. So make us laugh when you are preaching up there. And then give us something to think about." His father's name was Modesto – I call this the "Modesto homiletic principle"!

To face east, priest and people together, as some revisionists would like, does not convey a symbolic meaning as much as the sense that the priest has his back to the people (and is doing his own thing). By all means honor the resurrection; it is the culmination of Jesus' life that began in Mary's womb, continued in Galilee, seemed to end in Jerusalem, and burst forth again – everywhere – in the resurrection. And no, it is not that "his spirit lives." Nothing is more fundamental than to understand that he, the Risen One, lives - and in us.

The Mass is also called the Eucharist, and in Orthodox churches, simply the Liturgy. The prayers which most Catholics now hear and speak in their own language are those prescribed for the Latin rite which is the largest rite of the church. Many Catholics are unaware that there are other approved rites with their own arrangements of prayer. For example, at the funeral of Pope John Paul II representatives from the Eastern rites in communion with Rome chanted, after the communion, their special prayers for the pontiff and the church.

The Mass is also described as a sacrifice, renewing Christ's sacrifice of his life for us. One of the criticisms that some make of "the new Mass" is that the emphasis has shifted from sacrifice to commemorative meal. But what is meant by sacrifice? Many answers have been given, some stressing that it renews or repeats Christ's offering of himself in an unbloody manner, in the consecration of the bread and wine. But all this needs some discussion (which is given in a separate section).

The Mass begins, of course, with the sign of the cross, and then a greeting which paraphrases the greeting of the apostle Paul to his congregation in Thessalonika (this epistle is the oldest part of the New Testament). Then an improved prayer of confession, the song of praise (the Gloria), the scriptures and the homily, the creed and the general intercessions, all of which is called the Service of the Word. The eucharist proper begins with the offering of bread and wine. What follows is the eucharistic prayer, climaxing in the solemn offering (the doxology). All this is intended to stress an offering of the church, embodied in Christ, acting now through members of his body and empowered by the Spirit.

So the Mass is more than a communion service? Yes. It is an offering. And this is one way to understand how it is also a sacrifice. There is no more blood, no more slaying. The Latin words that mean sacrifice are "*sacer*" and "*facere*" - to make sacred or holy. Thus we seek in our worship to make holy - to sanctify - the offering of our lives, even specifically this day or past week. What is good is acceptable; whatever is bad (our failures, our sloth, our sinfulness) has already received God's forgiveness. There is much in a person's life, even for a single day, to offer. Sometimes it is an offering of pain or sorrow or disappointment, trials and upsets. Above all it is an offering of labor; the priest has already mentioned this in the prayers over the gifts of bread and wine and tithes. The work of our hands and mind. The care of children, the sick, the aged. The work we do every day. There can also be an offering of thanksgiving for the blessings received each day.

When the Mass in the past was not effectively shared as prayer, many people made the same kind of self-offering or sacrifice (making sacred or consecrating their lives) through private prayer. Now the liturgy gives this a new and solemn dimension. The priest says, "Pray, my brothers and sisters, that our sacrifice may be acceptable to God, the almighty Father." Is all this really the intention of the people in the pews? More or less. The Mass is a very rich prayer, and like all symbolic acts it is multivalent. Within the eucharistic prayer the most important element is called the *epiclesis*; it is the invocation of the Holy Spirit, and asks the Spirit to consecrate our gifts of bread and wine that they may become the body and blood of Jesus Christ. The priest is an instrument, not the direct cause, and in the past we often have not understood this role of the Holy Spirit. Why don't we ask the Spirit to consecrate the people? They are already consecrated, made holy, members of Christ's body in baptism. And they are here to unite themselves more fully, intentionally, with the priest. They are exercising their own share of the one priesthood of Christ. In the past we said little about this.

The liturgical reformers wished to lessen the emphasis on the consecration-elevation and place a new emphasis on the solemn offering. Thus the rubric was changed: the priest is to hold out, rather than elevate, the bread and wine after consecration. Many still elevate them, and to an observer it is obvious that there are now two high points in the eucharistic prayer: the consecration, and the solemn offering. Some have suggested that the rubric for the latter should be changed and everyone should pray together this final prayer of the eucharist (also called the doxology). Or that the word "Christ", not the pronoun, should be part of the text. The only role now given the laity is "the Great Amen" which is said or sung by all (and often weakly done).

We continue to need better and official eucharistic prayers, especially in dialogic form, and to think about a development which is rather startling to most Catholics. It is this: the church in 2003 approved for two eastern rites (in communion with Rome) their eucharistic prayers which omit entirely what we call the words of institution from the Last Supper. This needs study and explanation. But one recalls that John's account of the Last Supper also omits them, and stresses the call to service: Jesus washes the feet of his disciples and tells them to heed what he has done and do likewise. The Mass should always in a sense remain unfinished, because the work of disciples in bringing about the reign or kingdom of God goes on through time, perhaps all time, and certainly every day.

Where is Christ as victim in all this, and do we not, in the heart of one eucharistic prayer say to the Father, "See the victim whose death has reconciled us to yourself"? Yes, but.... Jesus as the victim, or the explanation of his death as a saving act - an expiation, an atonement - is increasingly debated by scholars who know that it achieved its full form and acceptance as given by St. Anselm in the 11th century. He was answering his famous question, "cur Deus homo," why did God become man. Other answers have been given – for example, the so-called exemplary model from Peter Abelard which stresses that Jesus became human to teach us how to live. And love. The first letter of John in the New Testament puts it thus: "One who claims to dwell in him must live and move as he lived and moved" (*1 Jn 2, 6*).

All this is appealing when one considers the heart of Jesus' message and his own example. It does not explain texts both in the Hebrew scriptures and the New Testament that seem to call for a victim, even an expiation, or give what is apparently a prediction that all this would take place and involve much suffering, according to a prearranged plan. This must be wrestled out by theologians. We read in the liturgy some of those problematic texts that imply the Father foreordained the sacrifice of his own Son, and it has often been compared to the demand made on Abraham to sacrifice Isaac. One of the more thoughtful answers to these texts that apparently "foretell" or prescribe Christ's death has come from a Protestant theologian, Ronald Goetz, who writes about this divine foreknowledge:

> **God simply will not accept our self-assessment as sinners enthralled by mortality and death. Christ's resurrection demonstrates finally the folly of our trying to ascribe ultimacy to sin, mortality and death. As the human parent looking through the**

eyes of love sees in the child a better possibility than could the stranger, so God sees us as better than we, as strangers to our own true being, can see ourselves. Unlike the human parent, God does not stand by helplessly as the child fails to realize its potential. Yet God does not enslave us in order to save us. God both has foreknowledge of his ultimate triumph and is intent on liberating his creatures. God's triumph entails the true freedom of humanity.

(*Christian Century,* 04/11/90)

The Real Presence

No words are more important in a sacramental religion, especially in the eucharist, than Real Presence. We dare to say that God – God in Christ – is present to us, and more than a memory. But is the meaning here something that cannot be rationalized, made real only by faith? We need a brief history of what the church has thought, and finally taught, about the Real Presence.

To raise this subject in the 9th century was the wrong time! Learning was diminished and the original understanding of "making the eucharist" was lost. A detailed treatment of this whole subject is given in *Jesus and the Eucharist,* by Tad Guzie. He tells us that a French abbot named Radbertus gives us "the first historical document we possess which examines the eucharist by focusing directly on the elements of bread and wine. The writing in the patristic period had centered on the eucharist as an action, not an object, not even a sacred object." But this new emphasis on what is the *host* continued. And the question soon emerged, if it is Christ's presence, *how* is he present? The answer unfortunately centered on a kind of physical presence which led to absurdities such as stories of bleeding hosts and an image of the infant Jesus appearing on the host. The considerable advance over this limited understanding (which is quite wrong - reality is more than physical) came from philosophy and with the recovery of Aristotle's writing on substance. Many Catholics immediately know what is next: the theory of transubstantiation, developed by Thomas Aquinas, which holds that the appearances of bread and wine remain, but the substance (the reality) has been changed to the body and blood of Christ. This was adopted by Trent and has remained the official position but it is increasingly questioned. Three articles on the eucharist in *Commonweal* magazine (10/7/05) present from one theologian a painstaking analysis of transubstantiation but indicate his preference for transignification, the Lutheran position which argues that indeed the physical properties of bread and wine remain but they now signify, at least to the believer, the Real Presence. Another contributor quoted the late liturgist and patristic scholar, Godfrey Diekmann, who said often and emphatically that it doesn't matter *how* the change takes place unless *you* are changed, and this is the important thing.

Because of the reformed communion ritual we are now well aware of the two meanings of the body of Christ: the consecrated host, and the baptized person receiving it. But the concept of the consecrated host as a sacred object not only persisted but led to an immensely rich devotional approach called the adoration of the Blessed Sacrament. And the reservation or keeping of it in church. And a special feast during the liturgical year, Corpus Christi, for which Aquinas wrote the sequence; it is long didactic poetry restating the doctrine of transubstantiation. It is a mistake to speak of this development in a dismissive fashion, even though it is so important to understand the eucharist as an action, and not primarily a thing. The reservation of the sacrament - keeping one or more consecrated hosts in the tabernacle - is familiar to every Catholic who also recognizes the red lamp burning as the signal of that presence. Moving the tabernacle to a special altar or shrine, apart from the altar of sacrifice or Mass, was not intended as a derogation but to restore the right emphasis. We must regain the personal and communal sense of the body of Christ. But to adore the Real Presence (Christ) has become over the centuries an obvious source of grace and blessings; saints and religious societies have sprung from it. And it can serve as an important reminder of the Incarnation, that Emmanuel (God with us) is really true. To understand the body of Christ in the primary sense - us, the people - is to emphasize that the divine presence continues in our flesh, not just in the bread, and in the world, not just in the tabernacle.

Can theology, with the aid of philosophy, really explain the Real Presence – two of the three articles in *Commonweal* were heavy going. Much more can be said than the way we explained for so long the mystery of the Trinity - "You just gotta take it on faith." Can we use the word "symbol" to refer to sacraments? Immediately some are uneasy because for so long we have heard the phrase, "only a symbol." But that way of dismissing or diminishing symbols is no longer valid. An example of misunderstanding is a poll conducted a few years ago by the *New York Times* that unfortunately is still quoted to show presumably how far Catholics have lost a sense of the real presence in the eucharist. The poll asked Catholics if (1) the bread and wine are changed into the body and blood of Christ, or (2) they are symbolic reminders of Christ. These are poor choices. What happens is more than a reminder. But symbol, properly understood, is correct. The consecrated host is both symbolic (a sacrament) *and* real. A symbol conveys a reality which is ongoing, or to which it still points.

For many people all this type of analysis is unimportant; "they just know" and it is simply regarded as a matter of faith. They are right on both counts. We have faith in Jesus and what the church and all its traditions have taught us about him. When he says to eat and drink this bread and wine which he called his body and blood, one does not have to be a deep thinker to understand this as a gift of himself. The scriptures assure us this is true. Think of the apostle Paul declaring, "I live now – no, not I, but Christ in me." Or one may read and really study all the references to the eucharist in John's gospel, after first learning that these are largely the faith conclusions of the early community of believers. They took Jesus at his word – or the meaning of his whole life and the Incarnation: God's self gift to each of us. It is now "localized" or brought very close in the sacrament.

The real difficulty is the inadequacy of words to explain what is real. Poets help, and here are four lines from John Donne, who reminded us in a famous passage that we are all part of each other. He said this of the eucharist:

He is the Word that spoke it.
He took the bread and broke it.
And what that Word did make it
I do believe and take it.

Reality is certainly not limited to the physical, and no one should believe that Christ's presence in the sacrament is physical. And that is why no one should go in a panic over accidentally spilling the wine (Christ's blood) or someone stealing and supposedly profaning the host. Thomas Aquinas said that if a dog should eat a consecrated host it is not the body of Christ. Long ago we needed someone with common sense to tell us that a wayward priest could not consecrate a whole bakery in some perverse action. No, it is not faith that makes this presence real; the reality or truth of the sacrament is the gift of God. But this is joined to faith. And the believer "just knows" that all this is real and true.

We struggle now in the new rite, and with frequent communion the norm, how to express this communion with God. Is it best done with silence? Song? With prayer? We use all of these.

The interval of silence prescribed after communion should not be omitted, even if we have great music.

Can the doctrine of the real presence be conveyed in an easier fashion - after all, we prepare children for first communion. I have tried, and will gladly defer to better catechists. Ask a child - call her Marie or Kate - to bring something to her mother that means or is a sign she loves her. The girl may produce a hand-written card. Or a flower. A present of some kind. Yes, these are signs of that love. We also call them symbols. A hug, a kiss or embrace, is also a sign of that love. "But your love is bigger than these." "Yes, this is what I mean!" Right on. (We are talking about meaning, truth, what is real.) "I love you, so I hug you. Or bring you presents."

"Well, Jesus loves you. And gives you a present of himself. It is called a sacrament – holy communion. He loves you so much he wants to stay close to you. Now think for a moment of why you eat." The answers here may vary! "Because I'm hungry." "I don't want to starve." "Mom makes me." "I love to eat!" You hope the child will associate eating and drinking with living, staying alive. With the gift of life. "It happens every day, Marie, that you eat to live. And to live happily, and be healthy. Well, God made the earth so that farmers could grow all kinds of wonderful foods which you eat to live. And enjoy. God made the grapes so people who are very good at it can turn the grapes into wine. Not just grape juice but wine, which is a grownup's drink."

"Jesus makes you a gift of bread so he can live in you! It is what we call a spiritual presence. People eat good things every day like bread and rice and maize to go on living. Jesus also gives you wine (perhaps later!) but some people in different countries have wine every day with their meals. Many people drink wine just to enjoy it. And Jesus wants to be a happy part of your life. Just think – in every Mass we have a gift exchange: we give bread and wine to Jesus, and he gives them back to us, but now he calls them his body and blood. That really means *his life.*"

I really don't know how one best conveys those words, "body and blood." I like to do it theologically – as many are coming to know, the Hebrew approach is that we live because God has made the gift of his own life in and through our bodies. All life in that sense is bodily life. Even with children, instruction can get heavy. The best line, I think, is "we eat to live. And Christ lives in you." We worry too much here about what is assimilated (a really good word). The problem, an old one, is that reality is greater than the physical and we don't have good names for that. The one most used, of course, is "spiritual," and it has to suffice but the word has lost much meaning, especially the noun ("spirituality"). We should reflect that if God is truly Spirit, and God is more real than anything else, then spiritual reality is more real than the physical signs of it. I wrote a communion song for children once in which the refrain is, *"Take the bread and the wine I will give you / body and blood I will give you / my life and my love I will give / Alleluia, Alleluia!"* It is the best I can do. Let the Holy Spirit (the gracious God) do the rest.

Questions and Doubts

We use the word sacramental, and I urge the proper recovery of the word symbolic. Words do have a history – or life-span. Not so long ago we replaced the Holy Ghost with the Holy Spirit! Even the old confessional prayer ended with "and you, my ghostly Father." Ghost as a word had become unreal. And in most cases to refer to "only a symbol" no longer fits, even though the novelist Flannery O'Connor made the phrase famous in a remark about the real presence that is simply now dated. Nowhere is this better expressed than in the French work by Gustave Martelet, *The Risen Christ and the Eucharistic World.* His first two chapters are titled, "On the Meaning of Symbol" and "Eucharistic Symbolism and Man's Condition."

Many have pointed out the words substance and accidents had one meaning four centuries ago and have quite another today, at least in physics or chemistry. One deep probing appeared in a letter in England's *The Tablet,* from David Peat, at the Pari Center for New Learning in Italy. He wrote:

> **A similar debate was held in physics when it encountered the mysteries of quantum theory. Einstein, for example, believed that the world must be constructed out of "independent elements of reality" and even Heisenberg initially believed that we could speak of the electron as "having" a position**

or a speed. It was Niels Bohr in Copenhagen who put a stop to all that. The notion of independent objects that "have" such properties is characteristic only of the large-scale world. There are, in fact, no "independent elements of reality."

As soon as we begin to speak about a "quantum reality" we enter into deep confusion and paradox because enfolded in our language are all manner of assumptions about the world (causality, space and time) so that "we are suspended in language such that we do not know what is up and what is down." Bohr favoured embracing complementarity – that is, holding together two positions which may appear paradoxical or opposed – for, after all, "while the opposite of truth is falsity, the opposite of a great truth is another great truth." There may well be fruitful parallels to pursue when physics and theology reach the limits of what can be said.

At a convent of dear Carmelite friends in Vermont I encountered "the crumb question" from a visitor who told me she had a friend who was concerned (she probably meant herself) about the crumbs that fell from the distribution of Holy Communion and did not seem to be gathered up with enough care. On a moment's spur and, I think, blown by the Spirit, I replied: "It helps to think about what bread is, and what Jesus was doing. Who would think of the crumbs as bread? Certainly not a hungry person. Not the boy making a sandwich. Not the grocer – he could not sell them. Not the farmer – he grows wheat. Not the baker – he shapes and makes loaves. The only person who would consider the crumbs as bread is the chemist who, if in doubt, might examine them under a microscope. And Jesus was not acting like a chemist at the Last Supper."

She was pleased with the answer, which I call a common sense solution. It goes without saying that we should treat the elements of holy communion with a proper courtesy, but the spilled wine on a rug is no longer wine in any functional sense.

Nor is it God. Or Christ's blood. Christ indeed was not a chemist but someone using a basic human ritual to bring us into not only a greater community but actual communion with himself. What we really should worry about is the decline of the meal as a major symbol of life together, helping us to understand the eucharist as, among other things, a sacred meal.

Journey to Emmaus

For another way to understand the key symbolic acts of our liturgy one should read often – indeed, learn and love – the gospel of Emmaus (*Lk 24:13-35*), about two disciples fleeing Jerusalem after the death of Jesus, bound for what they hoped would be a place to hide in the village of Emmaus, seven (some say twenty) miles away. Children love to act out this gospel, circling the table or classroom, putting on long faces (the disciples), Jesus waving his arms ("What's wrong with you two!") and deciding how he will "disappear" at the end – one little girl just dived under the table! They also have to run back to Jerusalem, only to be upstaged by the news about Peter's encounter with Christ before they can make their own great statement.

What does Luke's last sentence mean - "They knew him in the breaking of the bread"? Is all this another miracle story? Or is it the way they refer to a meal? To answer the easier question first, yes, it is a common way to refer to a meal. The expression even survives among us. We still say, "Let's break bread together."

As to the miracle question, it could be, but probably not, because the whole narrative appears to be written to teach us how we come to know Jesus in the liturgy – through listening to the word and by sharing a memorial meal. That summary leaves out some important elements – praise, confession, prayers, petition, thanksgiving, and above all the sacrificial action, the offering of Christ's body and blood, all of which is an integral part of the Catholic Mass.

Either the Emmaus gospel means something *historically*, as some would interpret it: they shared a meal and Jesus made himself known to them. And/or it means something *sacramentally*: we continue to know him in the eucharist, which was described very early as "the breaking of the bread." But again there is the question, how? Is knowing Christ in the eucharist explained by words like grace, a spiritual presence, the indwelling of his Spirit? And is "knowing" in this instance a matter of learning or experiencing?

These questions are all part of the mystery of God and the human, of how revelation works and grace is given. The ways of God with humans are many and varied. Yes, they may have taken the forms of visions, appearances, and miracles. And certainly they have taken the way of mystical intuition, divine grace helping an awareness that we could never attain by our best intellectual efforts. But is that all?

Historically. Sacramentally. Another way might be called "humanly." The way humans live, and interact, and speak, and love, and ground themselves in meaning which sustains their lives. This is what M.V.C. Jeffreys, a leading Christian educator during the 1950s, has said: "Religious truth is normal experience understood at full depth." The Emmaus gospel centers on sharing a meal, which Jesus did often with his disciples. It is normal to gather at a table, to talk together, to enjoy, to build up those bonds of family, friendship, love. It happens every day in families – or should. Food and drink on the table; friends and loved ones around it. This is not just how we go on living; this is life-deepening, enriching.

And it becomes depth experience. Rituals emerge; people have a special place. They belong. They are welcomed. This place is home, or at least a place of contentment, refreshment, and gladness. Because we eat, talk, and enjoy, we are living. And our sense of belonging is all part of a fundamental "longing to be" which means we cannot really exist without each other – if not this family, which will grow up and go away, at least we cannot exist without friends, neighbors, *society*. Sharing a meal, breaking bread together and much more, is all part of loving and living. It enters our memory poignantly. Later on we say, "Remember how we used to..." Special holiday meals are fondly recalled. And they are recreated in new families.

Reverse the statement: "Normal experience understood at full depth is religious truth." Are we not talking about the experience of what is meant by God? God who is the life giver, the joy bringer. The One who in Jesus promises life more fully, beyond all separation, including death. Are we not really longing for God in our longing to be one with each other, and are we not experiencing the presence of God now in our reunions, which foreshadow the day when we will be made one with the Father?

Jeffreys says, "What makes true religion is not that it relates to some abnormal field of thought and feeling." Does that mean visions and miracles? Isn't it harsh to say that these are abnormal? Yes, it is, but certainly they are out of the ordinary. And thus it may well be that in this story Jesus does not perform a miracle and materialize before the two disciples, like the image in a holograph. It says in the scripture not just that they recognized him but that "their eyes were opened." When *our* eyes are opened to see the deep significance of what we do together and what we are, we may see that God in Christ, God in his abiding Spirit and graciousness, is present in and through human life, and all creation. We do not have to be afraid of what is called pantheism. What we should fear is failing to understand mystery. Or the nearness of the One "in whom we live and move and have our being."

To say that one knows God, or God in Christ or the risen Jesus through sharing a meal, is not a new and strange notion that Christians invented. A passage from the prophet Jeremiah (*22:15-16*) seems to prefigure the Emmaus gospel, even to express the doctrine of the real presence more richly. It says:

Did not your fathers eat and drink,
and do justice and righteousness,
and then it was well with them?
They judged the cause of the poor and the needy,
and then it was well with them.
Is not this to know me? **Thus says the Lord.**

We say that this prophetic passage is even richer than the single line of the gospel because it implies that eating and drinking together – accepting gratefully the gifts of God which sustain our life - is for a purpose: not just to satisfy our own needs but to "do justice and righteousness," to "judge the cause of the poor and the needy." This is not only to know God but to help in bringing bring about the reign of God which Jesus taught and for which he came.

Intercommunion

Intercommunion is a persistent issue in Catholic theology and practice. At a Russian Orthodox liturgy I was refused communion, bluntly asked, "Are you Orthodox?" and I felt estranged, obviously unwelcome. The church for centuries has argued whether the sacrament makes for unity now, or points to an ecclesial unity still to be achieved. At the synod of bishops in Rome in October, 2005, the question was very much debated as to whether or not those divorced and remarried could be admitted to holy communion. The decision continued to be one of exclusion, although there was a definite minority dissent.

We have not achieved structural unity with churches such as the Orthodox, the Lutheran, the Anglican (in the United States called Episcopalian) and yet they believe as we do in the real presence. The sacrament for them and for us is not just "remembering" or "to remind us." Why exclude them from communion when they wish to receive and are sharing the Mass with us? Why indeed, when Rome itself at papal Masses has seen the pope himself give holy communion to Tony Blair, England's prime minister and an Anglican? And Cardinal Ratzinger at the papal funeral gives holy communion to Brother Roger Shutz of the Taize community? When pushed on the point, Rome says it is a special circumstance. Indeed, for the father who is not a Catholic but attends Mass with his Catholic family, it might seem even more a special circumstance.

An Anglican wrote to the *Tablet* that it was inconceivable to him that Roman Catholics and Anglicans could not take communion together, in the light of what Anglicans believe and pray. He is referring to the Prayer of Humble Access, centuries old and praised as a sublime composition. It says:

> **We do not presume to come to this your Table, O merciful Lord, trusting in our own righteousness but in your manifold and great mercies. We are not worthy so much as to gather up the crumbs under your Table. But you are the same Lord, whose nature is always to have mercy. Grant us therefore, gracious Lord, so to eat the Flesh of your dear son Jesus Christ and to drink his Blood, that our sinful bodies may be made clean by his Body, and our souls washed through his most precious Blood and that we may ever more dwell in him and he in us.**

We are not quite lost in a mire of definitions and disciplines. One shortcut some pastors use as to who should receive communion, especially at weddings and funerals, is to say to them privately, "If you are a Christian, and you believe in your heart this is a real communion with Jesus, that you are *in* communion, very close to the Lord by receiving this sacrament, then go ahead. Prepare yourself the way Catholics do (or we hope they do); put some meaning into the confession of sin and the Lord's Prayer, which says, 'give us this day our daily bread.'"

Since any New Testament scholar will tell you that we are not sure of the precise words Jesus used at the Last Supper (there are four accounts, and they are not identical), then we need a comprehensive statement. Such as: "I believe and hold most dearly that the Lord Jesus comes to me, invites me into communion with him through this most holy sacrament. And the Holy

Spirit, prompter of all prayer and goodness, has made Christ present in ways I do not understand (nor do theologians) but I am glad that Jesus thought of such a simple, gracious way to come to believers. To be their companion - 'the one who eats bread with.' Indeed he is present wherever love is present, but especially present in this symbolic or sacramental way."

There is room and even a direction for the celebrant to make brief initial remarks at different times in the Mass. The most familiar place is the introduction to the Lord's Prayer, and the beginning and end of the General Intercessions. Sometimes at Mass, before giving communion and proclaiming "this is the lamb of God," I quote the passage from Revelation which is applied to Christ: "I stand at the door and knock. If anyone opens to me, I will come in and dine with them, and they with me." Opening that door is the preparation one makes. But it is the Lord's initiative first, his graciousness to come to us.

Think of the 18th century heresy called Jansenism, which stressed the unworthiness of anyone to receive communion and taught this with such severity that its followers did not dare to approach the sacrament, except perhaps once a year, with great scrupulosity. It was Pope Pius X who lowered the age for First Communion to seven from twelve, an innovation that was widely resisted. It has taken a long time to persuade people that the communion is not a reward for being good but a help in the struggle to be good. The Pharisees once complained that, "This man eats and drinks with sinners." He still does.

The Mass as Sacrifice

Sacrifice, as we noted, is a word not easily defined, especially when we are told that the Mass is more than a commemorative meal because it renews in a sacramental way the sacrifice of Jesus on the cross. How to explain this is the subject of ongoing theological work. Certainly there are scriptural texts that support the understanding of the Mass as sacrifice; St. Paul says that "whenever we eat this bread and drink this cup, we show forth the death of the Lord until he comes." But what does that mean? We have a crucifix above or behind the altar. We have many books and heavy thinking on the subject as well as definitions from the Council of Trent and the 1993 Catechism. But the meaning is not easily conveyed, either to scholars or worshippers.

In popular understanding the word is associated with something difficult, often done because of heroic will or love that seeks the good of the other. For instance, "My parents sacrificed to get me through medical school." An older and pagan meaning of sacrifice is the offering of a victim - e.g., the killing of an animal in the temple and the offering of the blood to the gods - or God - as an expiation. "As I have power over this animal, you have absolute power over me." This type of bloody sacrifice by the Hebrews was going on in Jesus' time but ended after the temple was destroyed by the Romans in 71 A.D., and

Jewish leaders put together the present-day synagogue form of worship. Certainly a great many have heard and believe that Jesus paid a debt to his Father, a debt incurred by original sin and all sin, by freely choosing to substitute himself for us and then to die on the cross. But this approach has often dismayed people with the role assigned to God the Father demanding this kind of sacrifice. The concept of paying a debt for an infinite offense reflected the mindset of a feudal society. It is not acceptable today.

To speak theologically about Mass is difficult because of an embarrassment of riches. The Mass, for instance, is a meal but obviously symbolic or sacramental. Of what is it a sign? Of more than Jesus' actions at the Last Supper, but we begin there. Especially if it was the Passover meal, it commemorated the covenant God had made with Israel which made them God's people and led them from slavery to freedom, a real "passing over" or pasch. Jesus' language implies that this is now going to happen to him. He is the new Israel, and he will indeed pass over from death to life – and to glory. The result will be to summon and empower everyone to share his life, indeed, to become members of his mystical body. We begin to realize that the chosen race is really the whole human race; we are all the children of God.

For Christians the sign or guarantor and model of all this is Jesus himself, in becoming one of us, teaching the kingdom (and living it), and then passing through death to life and glory. And one further mighty deed: sending, with the Father, the Holy Spirit to bring us all into harmony, a true brother-sisterhood. The church at its best, and all of us, are meant to be signs of the kingdom, where justice and righteousness, love and harmony prevail.

All this may seem hugely intentional or short of achievement when we consider such horrors of history as World War I, fought for no good reasons by so-called "Christian" nations, and then in the 1980s the Bosnian War, a slaughter carried out by God-believers - Muslim, Orthodox, and Roman Catholic. And then the appalling instance in 1994 of the African nation of Rwanda, where eighty percent of those involved in the slaughter of 800,000 of their neighbors were baptized Christians, mostly Catholic.

I do not at this point call upon some unrealized eschatological future for a better world but invoke what I call the Gandhi principle, which he called soul force: it is the conviction, and indeed ready observation, that acts of love both heroic and ordinary multiply every day and keep most of the world sane. Without that "force" or power – think of God's grace and presence – we simply would not survive. And this is how the kingdom comes. We are asked to make a contribution and, beginning with baptism, our lives become or should become Christ-centered, Spirit-moved, gospel and church-guided, living icons of Christ still present in the world.

So the sacramental meal (the Mass) commemorates more than the supper, or rather, what the supper itself reenacted in the thoughts and prayers of those at the table. The passing over. The covenant or promise between God and people. Faithfulness – on both sides. Deliverance. Freedom at last. And now with Christ, even freedom from fear of death as total destruction. It becomes transition, and through all this Jesus becomes, as the gospel describes him, the Way, the Truth, and the Life.

All of this is built up, or should be, by the Service of the Word. And by our prayers and actions at Mass. We seek forgiveness. We pray for each other. We bring up the bread and wine. We greet or wish each other peace. These actions are important, they are the signs of Christ's body in its inclusiveness. No one should be left out. If sin estranges us, and someone feels this way very personally, the Mass is a time of forgiveness. Moral theologian Bernard Häring made that point very definitely. So do the Mass texts.

But a sacrifice? The word, as we noted, is historically laden with blood, slaughter, cruelty. In the chapter on Mass as an Offering I suggest one way to give a new meaning to the literal sense of the word: "make sacred." It is to sanctify the lives of those who offer the Mass, living under grace and guided by word and spirit, modeled and focused always on the One who teaches us still in the gospels, joins us to himself in glorifying the Father, and comes to us uniquely in the sacrament.

It is true that we can add nothing to God, but surely God accepts our way of speaking and doing in order to benefit ourselves. And others. We must think of Christ as present through all this, still teaching, promising, admonishing, and forgiving, encouraging. Acting as mediator in all our prayers and petitions, indeed, presenting us to the Father. Martin Luther made an expected objection to this approach of offering because it appears to seek salvation through works, not through Christ. But then he accepted this approach if Christ was mediator, the one on whom we lay our burdens and who speaks for us, because he was one of us, and still is

People no longer go in great numbers to Mass, let alone offer and participate in it. It is often said they reject the church. But we need to broaden our understanding of the church. It is hierarchical, yes, but essentially it is the people, the definition that came from Vatican II. It is the people who are temples of the Holy Spirit, living stones of the building, as Peter called us. When you put stones together you have a building, an institution. We recognize the necessity of church as institution and argue for its apostolicity, its more-or-less unbroken tradition. But we still struggle to realize the full implications of the church as the people of God.

A sacramental meal. A commemoration of the Last Supper. And more: the whole paschal event and covenant between God and people. But again the question, why a sacrifice? Because the new paschal mystery involves the gift Jesus made of himself (some would say dying on the cross, but that is only part of it). I would say the gift God makes to us in the Incarnation. And what that meant: Jesus' life and death. Then the further gift of the Father in raising him from the dead, crowning him with glory, and beginning a new creation. And the final gift of the Holy Spirit, coming to dwell within and empower each of us. This Trinitarian teaching on the love of God came slowly to the understanding of the fathers of the church, and is reflected in eucharistic prayers, called anaphoras, that began to appear in the 3rd and 4th centuries; they give much more structure and depth to the Mass than the eucharistic worship from apostolic times, and even the simple suggestion of breaking bread.

All this is foretold or alluded to by Paul when he speaks of "showing forth the death of Christ" each time we partake of the cup. And especially it is portrayed in the epistle to the Hebrews which invests Christ very much with sacrificial priesthood. But this has to be taken together with the emphasis that we all share Christ's priesthood, we are bearers of the Spirit, co-offerers of the gift. I recommend the chapters in Nicholas Lash's book, *His Presence in the World,* and other writers on the eucharist; they will, if patiently worked through, reinforce what has been said. But also it will make obvious the difficulty of scholars in explaining the eucharist. There are still the simple commands that come to us from the scripture, about body and blood. My life. Given, poured out. Do this to remember. "Re-member". And Luke writing even more simply, "They knew him in the breaking of the bread."

The difficulty is not only the usual weight of research; it is the nature of language, the words that fail the Word (but sometimes succeed notably). Think of those words or their meaning transmuted into music and all forms of art, into icons that invite the presence. And all the people, the communion of saints here and in heaven, in whom the Word has taken flesh. These living witnesses have come to us out of the great tradition; they have responded to the gifts of the Spirit, and when we encounter them in our lives, they are the real presence of the Risen One.

Shortly after I wrote this, the following letter appeared in *Commonweal* (12/2/05) from Joseph Amar, a Maronite priest at Notre Dame:

> **Your issue on the Eucharist (October 7) called to mind the efforts of Vatican II theologians to produce new models and language for the sacramental life of the church. The fact that traditional explanations of the Eucharist were weighed down by abstract philosophical language led thinkers like Yves Congar and Jean Danielou to turn to Eastern Christian traditions, and particularly to Syriac Christianity, for alternative approaches. Syriac authors developed a profound theological vision that was free of philosophical jargon. Their conscious choice to use the fluid language of paradox and metaphor allowed for a level of diction that was intended to short-circuit discursive modes of reasoning. Ephrem the Syrian, the most gifted practitioner of this method, speaks of God "putting on" human language to be known in Scripture, "putting on" human flesh to be known in our nature, and "putting on" bread and wine to be known as our food. These ongoing acts of God's presence are mediated through the Divine Spirit who moves eternally through creation and enlivens it. As Ephrem states: "Look! Fire in the bush that spoke to Moses. Fire in the womb that bore You. And now in the bread and in the cup, Fire and the Holy Spirit." This approach has less to do with *fides quarens intellectum* than *with fides adorans mysterium.* Again, in Ephrem's words: 'This Christ has come not to fill our minds with thoughts, but to bewilder our thinking.'**

By all means we should think out and discuss the insights in this remarkable summary. And Ephrem's "fire inspired" poetry should be better known in the west. He lived in the fourth century, and was a deacon and major theologian - and poet - in the Syrian church. He is rightly their glory, and Roman Catholicism caught up, so to speak, when Pope Benedict XV in 1920 declared him a Doctor of the Universal Church. Father Amar's final note about "bewildering our thinking" may dismay or be modified by those who seek clarity in prose and didactic statements, which come from such great teachers as Thomas Aquinas and are reflected in the creeds of the church. But Ephrem's approach to theology would be endorsed by another of the church fathers, Gregory of Nyssa, who said that "concepts create idols, only wonder comprehends anything."

Father Amar gave a longer statement on this method in an article in *Worship* magazine (9/87):

> **For Ephrem, the sacred is a dimension that does not submit to analytical investigation by the faculties of reason; only the more fluid logic of scriptural imagery is subtle and allusive enough to evoke it. As Sebastian Brock, a leading authority on early Syriac-speaking Christianity, has eloquently put it: "So astounding is the nature of the Christian mystery – God not just becoming Man, but becoming the very Bread for man to eat – that it is often more meaningful to describe this paradox in the language of poetry, where parable, myth and symbol can perhaps approximate to spiritual reality rather more successfully than straightforward theological description."**

We need both kinds of writing, and it should be abundantly clear that poets (and all the arts) must help us. If I wish to understand what the mission of the church is and how it defines itself, there are multiple volumes and dogmatic tracts but more often I quote a short poem by e.e. cummings that begins, "I am a little church." And when we stand in the light that revelation gives, one recalls the statement by Joseph Ratzinger in his book, *Introduction to Christianity,* that says in essence, when one has defined an article of the creed, it means that we have moved the mystery to another place to contemplate.

"Do This in Remembrance of Me"

The accounts of the Last Supper in the gospels should be closely studied to take note of their differences. But prior to these by at least a generation is Paul's account in *I Corinthians 11: 23-26:* "For I received from the Lord what I also handed on to you, that the Lord Jesus on the night when he was betrayed took a loaf of bread, and when he had given thanks, he broke it and said, 'This is my body that is for you. Do this in remembrance of me.' In the same way he took the cup also, after supper, saying, 'This cup is the new covenant in my blood. Do this, as often as you drink it, in remembrance of me.' For as often as you eat this bread and drink the cup, you proclaim the Lord's death until he comes."

Ask what was special about his death that we should remember it, and especially each time we gather for the Mass. There are different explanations, as we indicated; but there should be agreement that he does not approach death as a helpless puppet, and not because of a divine decree. I think the most fundamental answer is that Jesus died, as we do, because he was human, and mortal. He died violently and unjustly because he was a prophet. But again, what makes his death so different that we should remember it? A child might say, "Because he was God." The child is right. Not that Jesus knew his own divinity, but the meaning of the Incarnation is that God became, uniquely and incredibly, one of us. But again, why? Because of love. And if, for reasons that neither Job nor any of us can completely understand, we have been created subject to pain, suffering and death, even to so-called natural disasters, we need to recall that neither humans nor planets can escape limitations. We are necessarily part of a finite or limited creation. It is as if God said, "I will share all this. Share human life. Enter it in the flesh and blood of Jesus. And when death happens, I will share that but overcome it. I will raise Jesus, and then, with the help or gift of the Spirit, they will finally realize that he is the anointed one, the Christ. The Risen One who is still with them."

Thinking this way suggests that I should remember, at every Mass, Jesus' life, death, and resurrection; why? In thanksgiving. Because it gives grounds for hope that, as Paul wrote, "the last of the enemies has been destroyed." And to achieve holiness of life and further the salvation of the world. It is the reason that the priest stands at the altar, or table, and others come around. Jesus' life as God's spokesperson, as a teacher of the law, a law of love updated (think of the Great Commandment), a love that is focused and very specific – think of the call or command to be servants and to seek out the poor on the margins of society – all this is reason to join the commemoration of the total gift of God in Jesus which continues throughout time.

Once again, while the Mass is obviously a sacramental or symbolic meal which commemorates or remembers all this, Jesus himself that night was remembering the Pasch of Israel, the great deeds which God, who is faithful to the covenant (the promise), has accomplished in delivering his people. We still use the word covenant in the text of Mass; it reminds us that God keeps the divine promise and we who are baptized, who participate in this sacred meal, should be faithful also. Paul refers to the new Pasch, or passing over – from death to life. It happens every day until we "die into God," with whom, as Jesus said, there is no death – all are alive.

This explanation is rooted solely in God as love, and loving us.. The present Archbishop of Westminster in England said recently that we underestimate this love, forgetting that God is perfect, and if we use wonderful words to speak of human love at its best, what should we think of the divine love? It is love that brought Jesus to earth and flesh. It is the love described by the later prophets. It is the love so passionately portrayed in the Song of Songs in the Hebrew scriptures which reminds us towards the end that "love is a flame of Yahweh," a flame of the Lord "which many waters cannot extinguish." Yes - not even the tides of death.

Mass as an Offering of the Mystical Body

The Mass as the offering of the whole community is an understanding – and practice – difficult to establish after centuries of treating the Mass as the great work reserved for the priest, with the people reduced to the role of pious onlookers. Or devout Catholics who often prayed privately in any way they preferred. Golden treasuries of prayer, especially those with special rewards (indulgences) attached, were common; lay missals were not, although they began to multiply when the liturgical movement began to take hold. Indeed, by 1967 missals presenting both Latin and English, and Stedman's famous pocket missal, were everywhere. With the new reforms, especially the prayers in English (and presumably no more need now to read them in missals), the publishers were worried. A group of them in 1964 invited me to New York City to discuss the future of missals. I forecast a limited use in the future because already other publishers had sensed a new market and were producing en masse the missalette.

And Mass with people following along in the leaflet missals became and still is very common, to the dismay of some who point out that one does not "follow along" the script of a play on stage but listens to the actors. (And the Mass is not a play but a community prayer.) A "reading liturgy" seems to make a live speaker almost unnecessary. Some argue that they absorb the text better, especially the scriptures, from both reading and hearing. And how many lectors and presiders read well enough to be easily heard? It isn't just older people who have trouble hearing; a whole generation deafened by their music is now on scene. And many churches are poor in acoustics, partly because pastors and liturgy committees are not willing to spend money to make the church building a sounding box, a listening place (as well as a speaking and singing place).

A pragmatic solution is first to improve the reading skills as well as the amplifying systems. Purchase one or two good hymnals for the people (and if feasible use an overhead projector). Perhaps end reliance on missalettes but make available in the parish library or church store or the rear of the church the complete Sunday missal in English for those who have difficulty in hearing, or wish to prepare the Mass at home.

Any visitor to cathedrals and other large churches notices something now in disuse (beside most of the confessionals). It is the side altars that line the church or flank the main altar. The shift in emphasis to the Mass as a community offering - the whole Christ - has meant almost the disappearance of private Masses which, especially in religious orders, were celebrated each day by each priest. He was usually alone, although servers were sometimes provided (and always at St. Peter's in Rome). The server-acolyte probably did not know it but his presence was intended by the church to represent the community. And so, private or solo Masses are mostly gone, but allowed by way of exception for reason of devotion. It is difficult for some older priests to give up and re-think this great prayer and privilege.

Many priests have still not accepted the reform of the stipend. The names continue to be read or published "for whom this Mass is offered." Not so. It is offered for and by the whole community. The solution, slowly coming in, is to say in the bulletin or as part of the Prayer of the Faithful, "We commemorate – or make special remembrance today of ________________." People don't buy a Mass; they make an offering. And Mass cards in remembrance should use a different text to make this clear. It is difficult to establish this because the stipend is still part of the priest's income. One new memorial card says, "An offering has been made for the bread and wine of this Mass, remembering our beloved ____________________ and commending her to God."

The collection is now included in many churches in the offertory procession. It should be; it symbolizes many things. It has always amazed some Protestants to discover that Catholics take up a collection during church services *to pay the bills.* My friend who was a Presbyterian minister in our Kansas town told me in his church these were paid out of the budget. And the funds to meet the budget came from the pledges, paid monthly or quarterly, made by each church member once a year, at stewardship time. A committee called on people after the budget had been published. "Do you have an offering on Sunday?" I asked. "Yes, for the poor, and for various causes of social justice. We consider it our tithe to the neighborhood and the world."

An advantage to Catholics in adopting this system is that all our uncomfortable second collections could then become the first and only collection. Every Sunday the gift could be made not to meet expenses but "to deal our bread to the hungry."

In one parish where I "supplied" in the early 1970's, the pastor had the practice of soliciting names, just names, of the deceased, sent in with a dollar offering, not for remembrance on All Soul's Day but for Christmas and Easter. The names were to be read aloud during the sermon time. About one hundred and fifty. The same pastor would add to the preacher's words his personal greeting to the effect that "all you people are going to hell if you're not here next week - it's a mortal sin to miss

Mass!" Finally, to his credit (or mine) he ceased this crassness, or at least didn't do it at the Masses I offered. He was a hospitable man who once welcomed me back from illness with a great corned beef and cabbage dinner, and also humbly asked my advice on how to pray better. It's just that he had been ordained with no sense, not the slightest, of what the liturgy really meant. Pastoral work was mostly raising money and keeping up the plant.

There are other signs that the thinking that "we offer this Mass" is not yet fully established. Often the bread and wine are not brought up at daily Masses, and even on Sunday some churches neglect the table of offerings, which ideally should be set in the center of the church. And who brings up the bread and wine? Anyone, but it is appropriate for those who have asked for a special remembrance in this Mass, usually of a family relative they have given back to God. It is also fitting for parents at a wedding; they, with God, gave the gift of life to their children and now they see them at a nuptial Mass give themselves to each other. Symbolic acts have their own way of communicating. The bread and wine should come from the people; they are, as the two prayers after receiving them indicate, the gift of the earth and the work of our hands. Present the gifts, to join at last in the prayers of Mass, to offer and receive - all this is an expression of our share in the one priesthood of Jesus Christ. It is the epistle of Peter, not some innovation, which says, "You must be a holy priesthood, to offer up that spiritual sacrifice which God accepts through Jesus Christ" (*I Peter 2, 5)*. A few verses later he even calls us - all of us - "a royal priesthood, a people God means to have for himself." And Paul tells us to "offer our bodies as a spiritual sacrifice." Precisely. This includes but goes beyond martyrdom and a vowed virginity. Our lives are lived through the body. That is why it is so fitting in the funeral liturgy that the body is brought before the altar. The offering of one's life, the sacrifice, is now complete.

Co-Creators — "the work of our hands"

We offer bread. And the story of how bread came to be has never been told better (if you leave out God) than the account in *The Ascent of Man*, by Jacob Bronowski. The time: around 8000 BC. The place: the Fertile Crescent. Wheat only existed as something like grass. Then, in what Bronowski describes as "some genetic accident, the wild wheat crossed with a natural goat grass and formed a fertile hybrid." The resulting plant, called Emmer, had 28 chromosomes and a larger head which could toss off its seed; it was sown by the wind. And then "Emmer crossed with another natural goat grass and produced a still larger hybrid with forty-two chromosomes, which is bread wheat." The scientist calls this crossing improbable, and even more so, a specific genetic mutation in a single chromosome which made it fertile.

And so, the plant with the heavy kernel bearing the seed could no longer fling it into the wind. It needed man to plant it. And only a small part. The remainder our ancestors turned into bread. And still do.

The scientist calls this "a true fairy tale of genetics, as if the coming of civilization had been blessed in advance by the spirit of the abbot Gregor Mendel." Genetic accident. Fairy tale. Why there is any genetic mutation at all is not considered. The abbot and all believers in a Creator, more specifically a providence, see the hand of God here. We have been co-creators for a long time.

Often a poet puts it best; John Bannister Tabb wrote the following, titled "The Seed":

Still surmounting as I came
wind and water, frost and flame
night and day the livelong year
from the burial place of seed
from the earth's maternal bosom
through the root and stem and blossom
to supply thy present need
have I journeyed here.

But there has long been a difference of opinion among liturgists on the importance of bringing up the gifts at Mass. Previously the Offertory referred only to preliminary prayers by the priest made over the bread and wine which were either brought over from a side table or already on the altar. Some liturgists warned about overdoing this part of Mass because they wished, even back then, to emphasize the offering of the whole body of Christ at the end of the Canon. They warmed up to the argument by saying that no one makes a fuss over setting the table which, they said, is all that is happening here - unfolding linen cloths, arranging the chalice and the altar breads and the wine. But when this became an offering of the people, and they bring up the bread and wine from another table deep in the church, a new significance developed. The offerings become tokens or symbols of life and labor, as well as of God's providence. A popular liturgy has developed of bringing up other things, extending that symbol.

And a striking passage comes from Bishop John A. T. Robinson's little-known earlier book called *Liturgy Coming to Life*:

> **The offering of the bread and wine may seem like a mere preliminary action, like setting the table, something to get done, and done quickly. But from the earliest times, the presenting of the gifts was felt to be the special liturgy of the laity, their peculiar contribution which no one else could make. It is a movement that must have its origin in the very heart of the everyday world of work and leisure. It was 'as they were eating' that Jesus took bread from off the table. And in the offertory, the presenting of gifts, we are simply taking from the world a sample of the common livelihood of man - a loaf of bread and a bottle of wine. They are not native, uncultivated foods, or raw elements (as in Baptism, where the water represents the sheer action of God towards us, to which we contribute nothing). No, they are products; they are manufactures; they are signs of God's creation and man's labor upon it. Into that loaf of bread goes the whole working life of the world - all the complicated processes of production, distribution, and exchange. And in the bottle of wine we have the symbol of all life's joy and leisure, everything given to make glad and free the heart of man.**

The two new prayers which the priest offers when the gifts are on the altar are paraphrases of the Jewish *berakah,* a blessing on all created things. But this is also a time of music, and the rubric directs the presider to speak them quietly (a rubric that should be ignored when music is not present). The priest is making the same point when he prays that "our sacrifice may be acceptable." This part of the liturgy needs clarifying, a new structure of gesture and prayer. Above all we need to understand a spirituality of work as creative - indeed, continuing God's creation.

I have thought this way for a long time! In the 1960s in Colorado I gave a retreat at an academy for boys and I wanted to convey these points not only in words but by an added ritual. I prepared a small slip of paper, a quarter of a page, attractively written, with these four statements:

> …my REPENTANCE, for this past sin:
>
> ______________________________
>
> …my THANKS, for this special blessing I can think of right now:
>
> ______________________________
>
> …a GOOD WORK, that I did last week, and tried to do well:
>
> ______________________________
>
> …a GOOD RESOLUTION, a particular good work that I'll try to do well with your help:
>
> ______________________________

All this was unsigned, of course. What the students wrote, brought up and piled up before the altar was so heartfelt, so genuine that I kept these slips for a long time. They moved me to offer still another prayer for all those youths who are now adults of many years, and still engaged in offering their lives. I, the priest, remember all this; who among them remembers? But all efforts to enrich meaning are valuable. Someone wisely said that "all the Lord requires of us is that we make a contribution." We do that every day. Each day we can express repentance, and resolution, and thanksgiving, and offer our efforts at school, work, playground, home - anywhere. This was always the intention of the Morning Offering prayer; and offering the sacrifice of one's day (and life) supremely belongs in the liturgy.

The slip used at the students' Mass was headlined, in script, *"Lord, accept the gifts we offer. . . . "* And at the bottom, the line from the psalm: *"What shall I give back to the Lord in return for what He has given me?"*

Receive What You Offer

No single practice of the church at worship before Vatican II reflects how little the Mass was understood as an offering of the people in and with Christ than the method of giving out communion - when? Any time during the entire Mass. Especially this was true during Christmas and Easter when there were crowds to receive. Priests would pour forth, usually right after the sermon, to administer the sacrament. Why not, because the communicants had all made their semi-annual confession; they "stormed the altar" and only priests could distribute the sacrament (the ordination of deacons was a post-Vatican II development, and likewise the lay eucharistic minister). In this thinking the Mass, of course, was not something prayed or offered by the people but simply there to produce the communion (and, yes, the consecration-elevation). What was received had no connection to what was offered.

Another practice that still continues is to communicate the people with hosts consecrated at another Mass. For a long time and before Vatican II the church recommended that the faithful receive their own offering - the hosts consecrated at this particular Mass. Admittedly it is difficult to determine the exact number of communicants and in some cases the standard practice was for the priest to consecrate only his own altar bread and then move to the tabernacle and take out a large cup - ciborium - containing pre-consecrated hosts for the people. If one cannot have a Mass or is bringing communion to the sick, it is understandable to use pre-consecrated hosts. But to make it standard practice undoes the whole symbolic ritual of offering and receiving.

A practice that has disturbed some and pleased others is the baking and donating of "real bread" by parishioners. We have grown accustomed (in some places) to round, flat loaves which the priest visibly breaks and distributes, even though many other altar breads are needed. The breaking of the bread just before the communion is obviously an important sign. So, is all this pure gain? Not for some, because it leads to further worry about the crumbs. And the bread should not be imprinted with any kind of symbol suggesting Christ because the bread itself is the symbol of life and is now Christ's body – we don't need another sign to tell us. But isn't it supposed to be unleavened bread? Yes, and there are recipes that work for the home bakers but, as one bishop said of leavened bread, "If they believe it is the real presence, that's enough for me."

The Mass, then, is never finished, because the kingdom is coming. And the church was right to add the final line, "Go in peace to love and serve the Lord." Formerly the text was just dismissive, "Go, the Mass is ended." There are three formulas for dismissal; it is preferable to modify one and say, "*You* are the body of Christ. Go in peace to love and serve the Lord." Of all things, a priest was reproved for the way he ended his youth Masses. For the dismissal they all gathered around the altar. He said, "Go in peace, the Mass is ended." And they said together, "We are the Mass. It is our mission to go forth and be Christ."

The Eucharistic Prayer

The eucharistic prayer is the heart of the Mass and the subject of much discussion. It was formerly called the canon – the word means a fixed rule or norm – and there was only one canon for the Latin Mass. It continues in the vernacular as the first eucharistic prayer in the new missal. It is long and awkward, listing too many names, repeating a prayer for special intentions (which now take place in the General Intercessions), and has no *epiclesis,* the prayer invoking the Holy Spirit to consecrate the offering. EP I is not widely used. Of the next three models, the second is often used for the wrong reason: it is the shortest. It lacks any felicity of expression. Eucharistic Prayer IV is often not used because it is the longest. But it does express something of salvation history and Jesus' ministry, and our own calling for self-oblation ("that we might live no longer for ourselves, but for him"). It also expresses the role of the Holy Spirit in bringing about, through us, the fullness of grace. The wording is less felicitous after the consecration; in just a few lines the word "sacrifice" appears three times. Nevertheless we are called into "the one body of Christ, a living sacrifice of praise."

Both III and IV emphasize the bishops and the clergy; admittedly they - we - need prayer but one would like the laity, indeed, all humanity more emphasized. The second part of III improves on this. There are three EPs for children and they include a dialogic refrain. They are very appealing. There are two more for Masses of reconciliation. In many ways all these improve for Masses of reconciliation. In many ways all these improve on the standard four. But we are not done yet. Since 1973 there has been a so-called "Swiss canon," approved and translated into French, German, and Italian, and an English version approved in this country since 1993. It really is a "four in one" approach; the heart of the prayer is the same but it has prefaces and intercessions that relate to four themes; they are *The Church on the Way to Unity, God Guides the Church on the Way to Salvation, Jesus, Way to the Father,* and *Jesus, the Compassion of God.*

Agree or not, we should listen to criticisms of the new liturgy that come from people like the *Adoremus Society* who dedicate themselves to an elegance and correctness of style which they feel is often lacking in the liturgy today. With the Swiss Canon they raised doubts about how it ever got through. It is not in wide use and the language is not exceptional, but it has a refrain that involves the congregation. Such a litany, sung or spoken, is desired by many liturgists but not with the critics just mentioned. They see the priest as the one described in the Hebrew scriptures as entering alone the Holy of Holies. But a sung dialogic prayer can be a gracious expression of faith, signifying that the Mass is indeed the offering of the whole Christ.

To study and appreciate the eucharistic prayer one should study and pray one of the great anaphoras (prayer of thanksgiving) which come from the church fathers in the 3rd and 4th centuries, especially the one from St. Basil the Great, which is part of the Byzantine rite. It has a richness of expression; words are clustered like flowers – or expressions of love.

There is a single sentence from Denis of Alexandria in the third century that says much: **"The laity have three great privileges: to listen to the Eucharistic Prayer, to shout Amen at the end of it, and to reach out their hands to receive the eucharistic food."** Think for how many centuries we lost all that: the Eucharistic Prayer became the priest's own muffled business, and no one as a rule received communion, least of all in the hand.

The Symbolism of a Meal

A meal is so important as a deepening reality that the instinct is right to ritualize it, not only with prayer but place, and setting, and many other features. "We always have" is a sure sign of ritual. So is "this is my place." Others are more invented. There is the litany that begins "At our house we...." We do what? "We light a candle for anyone who is away." "We join hands for grace; sometimes we just say the Lord's Prayer."

"Let's eat" is another way of saying, "let's be one." One with food, and with each other. *Communion.* I can't "dig" you or eat you, but I can be *with* you, and we can be *in* each other in more ways than we realize. "Let's eat." It is easier to say and comes up more frequently than "let's love." But it has the same intention: to share life. To be one. One participates in symbolic actions like meals not just because we are hungry but to take in more of reality than the plate of food. The people who share this meal, and those who produce it, are entering my life as well as the food. Any bread, including the eucharist, that is broken and shared means that life is held out, made a gift, and gladly received. Communication becomes communion. We are not totally one. But we are "less two." We are less divided because we have shared a moment. And these moments are remembered in the days of aloneness, the all-by-my-one-ness which is ultimately the threat of death.

If we do not share meals together as a family or part of hospitality, there is no "transfer of meaning" to the sacramental meal where we share Christ. In our hurry-up and atomized culture this is a huge loss. We are the people who use phrases like "filling up," as with an automobile, and now hear from youth about "grazing," as with cattle in a field. For them it means moving from snack to snack in the mall. There are many books on food as an art – the French especially understand this – and the meal as the key symbol of extended family or hospitality; the Mediterranean cultures understand this. The family meal, where people are shared as well as food, where the day is reviewed and guests are welcome, is fundamental. It is put exceptionally well by Claire Davis, the daughter of the late English theologian Charles Davis. After her father's defection from the official church she said that her parents sought to find a more genuine and less institutional expression of their Christian faith. She herself found this best exemplified by the Catholic Worker community, but she recalls as fundamental the family meals at the Davis home. She writes of them (in *The Tablet*):

> **Our commitment to the Christian faith was not limited to explicitly devotional activities, or to a particular sphere of life; rather, it involved faithfulness to a path which encompassed the whole of our lives and which brought with it very real and tangible consequences.**
>
> **Predominant among these was the ministry of hospitality. I can, without exaggeration, say that I hardly ever remember eating a meal at home which did not include someone from outside the family. Intellectuals and students, individuals suffering mental breakdown and psychotic states, the lonely, the**

> **bereaved, and the confused all ate together at our table. My grandmother also lived with us for the last ten years of her life, requiring considerable nursing care which we provided as best we could. All manner of events and celebrations took place in our house, which was a centre of uproarious and chaotic life.**

One more apt testimony from the present pope, Benedict XVI. The Synod had just ended, October, 2005, and he had a farewell meal arranged for the 300 bishops. The menu was superbly Italian! At the end Benedict commented:

> **The Lord would not have chosen the image of a banquet as presaging heaven, if he did not approve of the beauty of a meal, of being together and eating together, and of the joy of the things of this world that he created.**

We must regain things which have been lost - the gracious (grace-filled) ways of living, and ordinary rituals which add to meaning. It was also well put by a letter writer (Ted Schroder) to a business journal; he said, "The trouble with homes today is not so much that they don't have the latest technology. It is that they have no kitchen table. No one has a place to learn we are all in this together. No one has time to confess - and to forgive." And more: "We are poorer, more broken and less able to be a family because somewhere we lost... our meeting place: our altar, our laughing, praying and being place. The kitchen table."

In the liturgy we are invited to participate in symbols of great realities—and the way life works. When we come to Mass, the assembly itself is the first sign (or it can be the beautiful church). The words, the music, the art, all the gestures of welcome. And in the liturgy, the breaking of the bread - the invitation of Jesus to "feed on him," to share this life-giving experience with others (of such variety!) because in him we are one.

It is this essential one-ness that furnishes the link between the liturgical life and the social teachings of the church. If we recognize the infinite value of each person, it should be obvious that there cannot be in any Christian's heart the corrosive attitudes of prejudice, race hatred, and the excessive forms of ethnical pride or nationalism. It is these evils which have so torn apart our society and fuelled our terrible wars.

The Way of Worship

When we define church in terms of creeds we do well to remember that the Latin word for creed is *symbol*, and what we express in a creed is by no means exhausted by the words; it is only positioned, so to speak, for reflection. All of us use signs and symbols every day to communicate; it is the way of being human, of being "in the body." And this could be one way to define church: **the church is a believing community that uses a certain set of signs, rituals, symbols, gestures, patterns of worship, and special words to express and convey what it holds about ultimate reality.**

But can this be put far more "existentially"? I will try, by summarizing the story of a cleaning woman told in *America* magazine in a beautiful essay by Katherine Byrne. This gifted writer found time from raising children to write occasional essays, and one of them was a reminiscence of Helma, a woman who came in to clean twice a week and left either the upper or lower half of their very domestic residence a thing of beauty and of joy for at least a few hours. She says of Helma that she finished the fourth grade and thereafter worked hard for other families all her life, worked on her hands and knees. What struck me, looking for illustration of the importance of symbols and music, was the story of her singing. Three hymns were her repertoire as she cleaned the house: "A Mighty Fortress," "O

What a Friend We Have in Jesus," and (from November on) "Away in a Manger." When Helma died, Katherine went to her funeral. Her pastor gave a eulogy: she would be missed, he said. She always made the coffee for the church social and washed the pews each spring before Easter. (Such are "the short and simple annals of the poor.")

Reflect on this a bit. Snatches of her hymns illustrate what philosophers mean when they say, in ponderous fashion, "the universe is friendly." Helma was not a philosopher; she just sang, "O What a Friend We Have in Jesus!" Theologians would tell us that the Word became flesh, and speak of incarnation, immanence. Helma sang a Christmas carol, "Away in a Manger." It was long ago in history, yes, but Jesus in the flesh, a baby who reached up to his mother's breast and who knew hard times, as she did. And the eternal One who came so close in the person of Jesus, such a God was and is powerful. Here the theologians speak of omnipotence, and say that the power of the universe is "graciousness," a "saving love," or some such language. Helma just sang, as millions have since Luther wrote it, "A Mighty Fortress is Our God."

She learned these hymns from her church, or Sunday school, or her parents. Hymns become symbols, and words pass over from sign to the deeper reality of symbols. Helma "participated in the symbol" (again the scholar's language) and so did Mrs. Byrne, when she reflected at the funeral that her cleaning lady was "safe within her mighty fortress."

Thus are the humble exalted, through their faith - and so are we, if we share that faith and that participation. We are safe, and in the heart of reality, if we open ourselves to the power of the sacred signs we use.

Participation and the Spiritual Life

If one reads all the great statements that praise the liturgy from popes and the Council, not just the scholars who labored so long to bring these riches to the people, there can be a disturbing feeling that it sounds *ex opere operato.* In other words, just offer the great Mass, sing the Divine Office, receive the sacraments, acknowledge the church year, and grace will come in abundance, blessings will flow, a purified soul and a holy people will be the result. Some of that is true; it is like standing in the sun and receiving the gifts of warmth and life. But this caution needs to be headlined: there must be an *internal* participation. Lending our voices in prayer and song must also involve the mind and the heart. A child would just say, "You have to mean it."

Precisely. And that is why there should be no opposition between various spiritual methods - Ignatian spirituality, pilgrimage, centering prayer, using a mantra, retreats, spiritual reading, meditation, contemplative prayer and all the rest - no opposition with the liturgical goal of full participation and forming one people, one Christ, praising and adoring God. The real cause of the split or misunderstanding is the individualism of our culture. "Myself alone with God" sounds attractive, but think of the Great Commandment which Jesus taught. And see the version by Luke, the first part of which is a whole-hearted focus on love of God, an absorbing form of worship we should strive for. But then the Teacher turns to love of neighbor, gives a compelling example (the Good Samaritan) and follows it with a command: "Go and do likewise." It is this understanding that we are a community which must be concerned for each other - feeding the hungry and much more - that led Dom Virgil Michel and others to insist that the liturgical life must lead to solidarity and commitment to the social teaching of the church.

The sick or enfeebled and the dying can do no obvious or physical good works. But look, they are part of a community, a very special one for which Pope Pius XII was the first to give the name, Mystical Body of Christ. It is now, with Pauline simplicity, just called the Body of Christ. Of this, all the baptized are members. We need each other; we minister and supply for each other. And to anyone, any fellow human. Of course – this seems elementary. But not when one considers how damaging has been the extreme go-it-alone mark of our culture. The terrible death toll in the great Chicago heat wave in 1995 (over 700) came about in part because so many, especially the elderly and the poor, lived in isolation and fear.

All the spiritual methods that Christians seek should aim at this end: to make us the family of God, the body of Christ, serving and supporting each other. How many people have responded at first to that famous but wrong definition of religion from William James: "Religion is what one does with his solitude." In the beginning of the liturgical movement there seemed to be a split between private spiritualities and public prayer. It must be harmonized. Put another way, we are not just in the business of personal holiness (or "saving souls") but bringing about the kingdom of God on earth. Or making a contribution. For this we were baptized, called to pray together, to offer ourselves in Christ in each eucharist and "feed on him - his word, his body and blood" in the sacrament now restored to us. Someone aptly corrected the old saying to make it: "Religion is what one does with his gratitude."

THE SERVICE OF THE WORD

Preaching the Word

Preaching is now considered an integral part of the eucharist and the sermon was given a new name, homily – preaching that explained some part of the scriptures just read. That often involves exegesis, meaning biblical scholarship, and it is only since 1943 and a landmark document from Rome, *In Divino Afflante Spiritu,* that the church has officially welcomed the work of biblical scholars. Before the renewed liturgy the sermon at Mass was often omitted or became a discourse on almost anything. Think of the angry phrase we sometimes hear, "Don't preach to me!" Preaching is supposed to bring good news, not bad news. The challenge now is to make it that other bread by which we live, remembering what Jesus said: "Not by bread alone does a person live, but by every word that comes from the mouth of God" (*Mt. 4:4*). To link the homily with the flow of the liturgy the old practice was ended of the preacher citing a text and making the sign of the cross at the beginning and the end. Put another way, the entire Mass is always a movement, or should be, from death to life, or towards a richer, fuller life as the children of God and the followers of Jesus. The Teacher said, "I came that you may have life, and have it abundantly" (*Jn 10:10*). The use of scripture, actually four passages in every Mass, and the word that follows are something to assimilate. Yes, like food. And this is, or could be, life-giving.

But there are major difficulties. The listener could say that the bible is confusing, a library not a book, a veritable mish-mash of literary genres. And no public speaker faces such a diversified audience as confronts a priest or deacon at a weekend Mass. It is no surprise that often he does not do well - and indeed, poor preaching is the most frequent complaint from a long suffering Catholic laity. There is no accountability here, and there must be. Confronted with a hopeless or ill-prepared preacher, some of the congregation read books or the bulletin. Or exit the church - two American visitors did that in London when the priest, after reading from Genesis, said it is obvious that women must accept a secondary role because they were created after the man.

There would be a considerable reform if people not only had a voice in choosing a new pastor but heard him deliver a qualifying sermon. Or two or three - as many Protestant churches do. Yes, we are a hierarchical church but the big difference now is that the laity are educated. There is nothing "apostolic" - only the wish to control - that keeps parishioners from approving the appointment of their pastors and preachers.

I do not accept the frequent assertion by Catholics and uninformed journalists that preaching in the Catholic service is subordinated to the eucharist and hence less important than the action of the priest at the altar. It is "all of a piece"; he is ordained to preach the word as much as to preside at the eucharist, and his training to do so is usually deficient. There is no greater need in the Catholic church (and in much of Protestantism) than to achieve an adult understanding of the faith. What good is biblical scholarship if we remain like children, mired in fundamental or literal understanding of the scripture? Fr. Raymond Brown has said, "It may well be that many priests trained before the 1960s have never even heard of the 1964 Biblical Commission Instruction, and so do not know what the church is now teaching about the gospels, while those trained in and after the 1960s have little knowledge of the ultra-conservative views previously taught in Catholic seminaries." It was this Commission that said the divinity of Jesus was not clearly perceived until after the resurrection. There *is* real progress in replacing this fundamentalism (or ignorance); parishes now have courses on the bible, lay people study in theology schools, and read books.

The proclamation of the scripture, except for the gospel, now involves lay people who are lectors; this is actually a minor order, like acolyte, and both are conferred on candidates preparing for Holy Orders. To older Catholics it was astonishing - and for some, upsetting - to see lay people step up to the lectern or pulpit and read the word of God. Some old-time pastors actually forbade women to take on this role (or that of eucharistic minister) until they were ordered or shamed into doing so.

But in general the reading (which, remember, is a liturgical act) is not well done. This is true also of the priest; recently in Stratford on Avon, the Canadian city famous for presenting the plays of Shakespeare, I listened at Sunday Mass to a really poor reader and preacher, speaking rapidly in a flat, toneless voice, and thought of the extraordinary talent which actors develop in using the gift of language, of speech. We need some of the same training.

This deficiency showed up early in the transition to English; listen to Maisie Ward (of the famed Catholic publishing team, Sheed and Ward) in an article in *America* (5-30-70):

> **If the English liturgy is to be fully successful, no priest should be ordained and no reader allowed to read who has not received this order after training and testing out in a large building. Talk not of microphones: the readers either put their mouths so close that the buzz makes them still more inaudible, or they turn to one side or the other of the mike**

> **or else talk over the top of it. And no one (I include myself) has the courage to tell them how inaudible they have been. I know only one church - Westminster Cathedral - where the administrator has a class of readers in training.**

She does say that she heard an excellent reader – a woman – at a Mass in a school in Chicago, and tartly observes, "Very few churches are enlightened enough to prefer a literate woman to an illiterate man!"

That was 1970. And still, much public reading gives no life or lift or timing to the words. Liturgy commissions, especially at the diocesan level, should hire professionals and share the expertise among the parishes to train the readers. It should be considered just as important as hiring music ministers. And lectors should qualify; if they do not read well they can be directed toward other forms of ministry. There are or should be rituals for their installation, and for lectors surely one should incorporate a few lines about the lector called Ezra in the book of Nehemiah. The Hebrews were overjoyed at their return to temple worship and it says of Ezra the lector that he "stood on a wooden platform higher up than any of the people and read plainly from the book of the law of God, interpreting it so that all could understand what was read" (*Nehemiah 8:1-3*). (Some lines in this passage we need not heed; it says that he did this from daybreak till midday!) Another biblical verse to quote should be held out as a goal for all who read. It is the word from the prophet Isaiah which we hear on Passion Sunday: "The Lord God has given me a well-trained tongue, that I might know how to speak to the weary a word that will rouse them." (*Is 50:4*)

For installing all parish ministers, nothing is more fitting than Paul's first letter to the Corinthians:

There are different gifts but the same Spirit; there are different ministries but the same Lord; there are different works but the same God who accomplishes all of them in everyone. To each person the manifestation of the Spirit is given for the common good.

(1 Cor 12:3-4)

Many ministries but one spirit. Readers as well as preachers should be heard and judged capable. If it is difficult for fellow parishioners or pastors to do this, let the speech coach hired by the liturgy committee do it. Recommendations like these, of course, are the stuff of dreams; in many cases people are just asked or volunteer to read. A program of qualifying and certifying those who read goes along with reevaluating greatly the word and those who give it.

And the really great readings that appear in the lectionary, such as the two passages on love from St. Paul (*1 Corinthians 13* and *Romans 8*), or the Beatitudes, should be awarded to the best reader, not just those who have the next assignment. A reading can be a work of art as well as a proclamation. It should be. We are a long way from the "declamation," when people gave public readings or passages of great poetry. For an example, see the film, *The Dead* (John Huston's last opus), set in Dublin in 1912. One of the guests at the Epiphany party reads or gives from the heart a prose passage, and does it so well that the listener is privileged to hear. And is changed.

Problems with the Lectionary

There are problems with what is read as well as the reader. The most glaring fault is the anti-semitism expressed in the New Testament. Some would argue that this problem has been identified; the church has officially repented; conferences are held between Jews and Christians for better understanding, and there has been since 2000 a Center for Jewish-Christian Learning at Boston College. So what is the problem?

This: the offending passages are still in the lectionary and read on both Sundays and weekdays. And more than anti-semitism; an author writes in the *Journal of Biblical Literature* that "the Muslim extremists who attacked the World Trade Center and Pentagon took their inspiration from the Qu'ran, but they could have used the Bible," and notes that during the Israelites' conquest of the land they were directed not only to overcome but also to destroy all the inhabitants (*Deut. 7, 1-6*). There are other passages that command us to care for the aliens in our midst, but the "texts of terror" were cited to justify hideous passages of history deemed righteous by their perpetrators, such as Oliver Cromwell against the Irish Catholics, the Puritans in the New World against indigenous peoples, white South Africans against blacks, and Zionists - both Jewish and Christian - against the Palestinians.

But surely it is the task of the preacher to put the text in context, and to convey to the congregation the understanding we now have, to correct the misinterpretation that has prevailed for so long. Indeed this should be the solution but in most cases it will not happen. Why not?

Consider the structure of the Sunday Mass/liturgy. There are three scripture passages proclaimed, plus a psalm. Is the preacher to comment on each one? Can he do that in the fifteen minutes which is the most time usually allotted to a homily in Catholic churches, making it compatible with the rest of the liturgy? And in many cases the preacher is ill-equipped and ineffective.

The answer is not to abandon the New Testament because it has anti-semitic passages, a solution that has been wildly suggested. Should the readings be improved, the lectionary revised? Yes. What was accomplished after the Council was a great gain but it is time for revision. That will take a long time but there is a corrective that can be put in place right now. **It is to require that all scripture readings in the liturgy be prefaced by a short (three or four lines) expert commentary. In other words, a brief exegesis before the reading. Each reading.**

Will this make the liturgy too wordy and too long? This is a danger. But the other danger is to leave the scriptures unexplained, and allow the ignorance and misunderstanding to continue or be reinforced. Why not settle for printing such learned summaries, both helpful and clarifying, in the parish bulletin? Agreed, if people read the bulletin. They *hear* the scriptures at Mass. We should do both.

Considering the time problem, one solution is to omit the second reading, which is permissible, and the practice followed in Germany. One hesitates, considering how long it took to have a genuine Service of the Word in the Catholic Mass. Continue the readings for now, but face the fact that we cannot continue to do great harm proclaiming the unexplained texts. There are too many passages that add to prejudice, confirm ignorance, and are injurious. This is true in more areas than the problem of anti-Semitism. Here are some examples. The condemnation of divorce in Mark (this passage begs to be put in context). The presentation of a warrior God (made in our own image), ordering the slaughter of his enemies. The references by Paul to the opposition of flesh and spirit (by flesh he does not mean the body, as most assume). The passages in John that imply an exclusivist view of salvation. The cultural limitation that colors the descriptions of heaven, hell, judgment, eschatology.

The daily readings present a similar problem and in some respects are worse. These too call for immediate remedial action. The word of God should not be the source of misinformation. The old prejudices and animosities that influenced the text should, like weeds, be cleared away. The message of the Holy Spirit will come through when the limitations of the authors and of the times are explained.

MUSIC IN THE LITURGY

Music in the Liturgy

Of the many books on reforming the church after its great scandal, stellar reviews went to *A People Adrift*, by Peter Steinfels. In his chapter on liturgy he says this about music, especially congregational singing:

> **Music is perhaps the weakest link in Catholic worship today. The problem is not that some, maybe much, of the music is an affront to good taste, although that is true. The problem is that the worshipers don't sing, and when they don't sing the result is worse than if they had never been expected to. Imagine a birthday celebration where two or three out of ten family members actually sang "Happy Birthday" and the rest stood silent or barely moving their lips. What would be the message? The ragged, halfhearted, dutiful singing that marks so many Catholic Masses is more than a lost opportunity; it is a distinctly dispiriting experience, a positive obstacle to worship. Those few with strong voices don't know whether to stand out as quasi soloists. Those with uncertain voices hesitate in the absence of a collective sound into which they can blend. Catholics are not unaware of the widespread failure of their sung worship - but by and large it is treated as peripheral.**

Is this too strong an assessment? No, and it could be different. Catholic musicians have their own association and when they meet it is like the great Masses of the Liturgical Conference all over again; the song and prayer move the soul. And there are a few parishes which are musically proficient. They have pipe organs, decently paid choir and music directors, and well-trained choirs. There is a struggle with classical liturgists who want people to sing the Mass prayers and not just the usual four hymns which are now common at the beginning and end, the offertory and communion. They have a good argument, and the best solution is to combine elements of both. In Germany for a number of years I have been fortunate enough to visit my friend Irene Lückert at the time of the Pentecost Mass, and we go to the Jesuit St. Michael's Church in Munich. Music is very important, and the Mass on this major feastday is always one of the great classical compositions, sung with a large choir and orchestra. This is not just a performance. Germans really sing hymns, and a hymn at the beginning and perhaps at the end are included, along with Mass responses. The large church, handsome in rococco style and with no pillars to block the view, is crowded with people who begin arriving an hour before. One year there were sixteen various ministers involved in the Mass, and not a single woman. But that has changed, and altar girls and female lectors are now present. (So are thurifers - finally someone succeeds in making incense!) It is a glorious experience of worship, especially for a feastday largely unappreciated in the United States and in Catholic understanding.

At the time of the Reformation it was said, "Let them sing and they'll be Lutherans!" In answer, German Catholics began to sing hymns that accompanied or interpreted the Mass – at least these could be in the vernacular. A pleasing episode happened in 1944 at a German prisoner-of-war camp in Missouri. Father Bede Scholz from Conception Abbey was asked to go to the camp to offer Mass for German prisoners who were Catholic. To his delight and surprise, as he began the Latin they broke out into vigorous song.

But what about back home? At every Mass the priest says, "Lift up your hearts!" And we respond, "We lift them up to the Lord." But still the truism: one thing we don't lift up, for the most part, is our voices in song. Is it really hopeless to expect that Catholic parishes will ever sing, really sing the Mass and the hymns? So much effort, so many mistakes and small gains. If you wish to know the state of Catholic music, visit around, and then go to some Protestant churches for comparison. Check out a really fundamental point: can you hear well? The spoken word, of course, as well as music. The building as sounding box should be a prime consideration. What is the state of the amplifying system? And why is it used at all by soloists who have well trained voices? A prime question: what is the quality of the organ? Is it a pipe organ or electronic? In Germany you will find a pipe organ everywhere, Catholic or Lutheran churches, large or small. Continue your search over here and ask: is there adequate funding for music ministry, including a professional salary for the organist/music director and funds to support the whole program? Even some parishes with high income and highly educated people falter here, and wind up making do with a poor electronic organ.

All this is well known to Catholic musicians; we just don't show many results. Name a single hymn that all parishioners know by heart (or all Catholics everywhere). Perhaps the first verse of "Holy God We Praise Thy Name." The first verse of "Silent Night," and perhaps one other Christmas carol. (Where are the carols for Easter?) One expert and weary veteran of directing and improving church music, Randolph Nichols, has told me that we need to emulate the Baptists in learning thoroughly about thirty hymns that they frequently use. Provided they are good hymns with good text, what a treasury we would have. But the text of many hymns is bad theology, poor poetry. Nichols also challenged me to follow up on St. Augustine's oft-quoted remark, "He who sings prays twice" (the correct translation is "he who sings *well* prays twice"). He said if this is really true, why doesn't a parish organize instruction in singing - beginning with how to read music and sing in parts - and prepare people not to join choirs but to pray well. This would be supplemental to the choir. He produced a six-week course and it was published in *Good News,* but there was no great demand. Remember, we are a society where people no longer gather around a piano - or a banjo, violin, or guitar - to sing together. We listen to music, yes; sing, no. In a pre-tech society it was not so. The Welsh still sing. The Irish sing in pubs, not much in church. In monasteries a schola or small group often acts as a second conductor or support for singing the Mass. "Praise groups" serve the same function in some evangelical churches. We can do the same.

The cause is not lost. Some parishes have remarkable music programs, and "pack them in."

Go to Rome and in the Trastevere section find the beautiful old church of Sant' Egidio. Thomas Cahill found it, and concludes his book on Jesus and the gospels (*Desire of the Everlasting Hills*) with five pages on the Sant' Egidio movement, the lay apostolate now spreading everywhere (and for many, a great sign of hope for renewing the church). They sing. Cahill writes: "The prayer is the most beautiful I have ever heard, modeled on the sonorous chant of the Russian church and sung from the gut with reverence and feeling. Each night they choose a theme: on Monday night, for instance, there is" "Prayer with the Poor," on Wednesday "Prayer with the Saints," on Friday "Prayer at the Foot of the Cross."

I have been there three times, and *this goes on every weekday night.* They won't give you their adaptation of the music, but encourage you to find your own, and they help new groups with themes to pray and sing about. At the ecumenical monastery of Taizé in Brittany, France, the single one-line melodies in different languages enable huge crowds to pray. At the memorable funeral of that great shepherd, Joseph Bernardin, Archbishop of Chicago, the cathedral echoed beautifully with the Taizé chant, "Jesus, remember me when you come into your kingdom."

Monsignor Martin B. Hellriegel was one of the true pioneers in the liturgical movement; his achievement in music and full participation in the Mass led many to visit his beloved parish, Holy Cross, in Saint Louis. In explaining his approach he quotes his prime text, from Pius XII's *Mediator Dei*, #192:

> **Indeed it is very necessary that the faithful attend the sacred ceremonies not as if they were outsiders or mute onlookers, but let them fully appreciate the beauty of the liturgy and take part… alternating their voices with the priest and choir, according to the prescribed norms.**

He began with hymns and then taught first the children and then the adults the Gregorian chant Masses. There were two choirs, men (no mention of women!) and boys, and they were placed in choir stalls between altar and congregation. He recognized the abuse of the requiem for daily Mass that I have mentioned. In too many parochial schools children were marched into the choir loft to sing a requiem high Mass with the same dread melodies and that dire sequence rightly named the *Dies Irae*. For him the solution was to persuade people to accept daily sung Masses and the proper readings and prayers of the day.

Several times I experienced another service there, the singing of Compline in English by the children, alternating with the congregation. Compline is the church's goodnight prayer from the Divine Office. It was a moving act of worship and inspired me to labor over an English translation of an Advent novena booklet which used the O-antiphons and chant melodies. The omission of women from the choir was probably considered more liturgical, following directives from the same Pius X. It seems incredible now. And there is the problem of understanding; the Mass was still in Latin and these were children of grade school age. Choir boys in English cathedrals all these centuries have sung in their native tongue. Mouthing Latin by altar servers and boy choristers is surely not ideal. But what is ideal is a sense of beauty, propriety, form and great dignity. And this the learned and stately pastor imparted; Hellriegel knew liturgy well, from his German background and from years as chaplain to the Sisters of Most Precious Blood Convent at O'Fallon, near St. Louis; they were so attuned to the liturgy that they actually experimented with the Easter Vigil in the hours of darkness where it has always belonged. He loved what he did, and communicated that love in his fatherly way. His parish in those days was an example of what could be done today—in English - except that there are not many Hellriegels.

The Official Neglect of Music

Some who have studied the work by the scholars who produced the reform (the *Novus Ordo*) have said that there was a rather astonishing lack of attention to the music problem. The vernacular was a great gain but what would replace the Latin chant Masses and the singing of the Divine Office? In England there were good composers who labored mightily to produce Masses and the Divine Office in English. And in France both Gelineau and Deiss produced a psalmody, quickly translated. But everywhere the so-called folk Masses burst out with instrumentalists, mostly guitar players, leading quickly written songs. Undeniably there was enthusiastic participation; young people jammed these Masses. The flimsy pop music in early years was improved with compositions from the Weston monks and the St. Louis Jesuits and others. But the argument continues over quality, aesthetics, and the permanence of these compositions. They succeed in participation, yes - is that enough?

The music scene is a paradox: on the one hand: you have organists, musicians, composers, and choir leaders who use their considerable talents in praise, in the service of the liturgy. With all this talent and dedication, why is there such a lack of good singing at Mass? And no widely accepted sung Mass in English for the proper prayers (the Gloria, Sanctus, etc.)? One reason is that there is no effective way to voice opinion, maintain quality control. Each diocese has a liturgy commission; few of them visit parishes to issue a critical review of the liturgical action (including preaching). And few parishes have taken the suggestion to provide a "book for comments" at the entrance of the church. Perhaps only then one will hear such critiques as the pace set for hymns is too slow - or too high, or too fast, the organist too loud, drowning all attempt at congregational singing, hymns deficient in both words and music, or unfamiliar, a soloist who overpowers us with the microphone, and so on. It is indefensible that there is little or no assessment of what we do each week, our most important hour. Steinfels in his book notes that the *New York Times* makes this kind of critical review *for each issue.* Look: even though attendance has declined, the eucharist is still the principle religious activity of any Catholic parish. "What can we do better" should be a question raised after each weekend of prayer and praise.

Another reason for poor music: there is still a lack of money in the budget for the music ministry. Catholic universities like Boston College and Notre Dame give scholarships to students who can play football and basketball - you bet they do. They could also recruit in Catholic high schools for those students who are leaders in worship, who would be good liturgists and musicians. Guitar players, yes, but more. Despite the need for popular participation there is a large contribution that soloists and superb instrumentalists can make. Over the years I have heard this at Masses directed by a great church organist, Timothy Zimmerman. A flutist or a violinist, usually playing at the offertory or communion, or the organist himself, or a highly trained singer can produce absolute stillness in the congregation, and occasionally an outburst of applause, which in general is not recommended but on some occasions is unavoidable. The talents of great performers should not be restricted to concert halls or weddings.

SACRAMENTS

A Poetic Summary

Let me begin a discussion on sacraments (four of them) with a poetic essay (the influence of Ephrem the Deacon!).

Catholicism is very much a sacramental religion.
This means more than the seven sacraments.
It means all things are signs.

Think how many small actions are repeated in daily life.
If we know how to read them
we would understand that they are often pointers to God.
They point beyond themselves
to the mystery of being,
to the giver of meaning, and the source of life.

Take the daily round of eating, drinking, sleeping,
waking up or rising up to a new day.
Think of loving, making love, making children,
of working and creating.
And speaking. We speak millions of words in a lifetime
and many of them, thank God, do make sense.
Language is not merely a convention.
The capacity for language, and meaning itself, are gifts.

Sometimes the words we speak – and hear, or read –
point us to Wisdom, or Truth.
And these are other names for God.

Think of eating and drinking, those delightful activities
which the Creator planned for us to do every day.
How often Jesus ate and drank with his disciples!
Why does he come to us now under the signs of bread and wine,
bread that is broken, and wine that is shared?
Because food and drink give life,
and all life is from God.
All life is for God.

And our life is not mere existence, a kind of dragging around.
It's not bread and water but bread and wine
that Christ chose to signify (to be signs, or sacraments)
of the life of God we share.

Baptism

It is gratifying to see baptism become a real celebration; the argument continues as to whether it should take place at Sunday Mass so the community can welcome its new members. This impacts the time frame and especially the homily. I think it is preferable to introduce new members by name or in person at later Sunday Masses. When a pioneer catechist, Christiane Brusselmans from Belgium, labored heroically in the 1970's to introduce the RCIA (Rite of Christian Initiation for Adults), few predicted its success. But many thousands have sought out the Catholic faith through the RCIA, and it has given a new significance to the Easter Vigil, when ideally these adult baptisms take place.

When biblical scholarship began to be recognized in the Catholic church, and it was possible (or safe) to explain the Genesis account of the creation and fall as religious myths, a new understanding had to develop concerning original sin. Such as? The evil that originates in a society or culture into which the child is born, and which he or she must resist, with the help of grace and the Christian community. Or perhaps, as some now argue, a genetic mutation that inclines us to violence and discord. Dennis O'Brien, the noted author and educator, has argued that through baptism the child is born into history - at a particular time and place - and he or he is now called and empowered to help shape that history according to the pattern which Jesus called the kingdom of God. To that end we hear the gospels, learn of Jesus, and in our own circumstances live his life. I first met O'Brien through an article in which he said the reason there is no "life of Jesus" in the gospels (or standard biography) is because we who receive the Spirit and become through baptism members of his body are to live that life in the world - in our own special circumstances. "All that God expects is that one make a contribution." A few examples of the Christ-life that begins with baptism, the birth into history: our whole history of violence, especially now, should certainly impel the Christian to be a peacemaker. And the millions who still live in brutal poverty and near starvation, the poor in a world society which is rapidly becoming very rich and very poor, should certainly influence our calling, commitment, and lifestyle.

Administering the sacrament needs to be enhanced. The ritual needs better texts, music, and song. The renewal of vows at Easter Masses should continue, but perhaps there should be a personal renewal on the baptismal anniversary (if indeed one remembers it). Who keeps and brings out the baptismal candle on those anniversaries? Or for the family meal (if there is one)? At a recent baptism in a Manhattan parish I found the font to be no more than a saucer; no shell ("just dip your fingers or cup your hand, Father") and no paschal candle in evidence at all. No white garment (which in fact is redundant). No exorcisms because "they can be omitted."

It is possible to improve all this. Somehow incorporate the Bible into the ritual; the child might be persuaded to place his hands upon it. At least bless the child with the book. If there are siblings, let them prepare posters or decorations. Learn the Hail Mary, to say publicly for their new brother or sister. Reach up to light the baptismal candle for the baby from the paschal candle. And write a prayer - parents sometimes write a letter to be read when their son or daughter leaves home, perhaps for college. Someone should hold up the child to God, like the African custom in a naming ceremony. All this is a happy but sublime occasion; creation and God's gift is never more evident than in the conception and birth of a child - which is also why there should be a time of silence to reflect on the mystery of life, and God's love.

But when should "infant" baptism take place? No longer the rush to the font under pain of mortal sin. A practical rule, then: before they can walk. A friend had one baby "reverse the symbolism" of joining the church by squirming free and running out of the church! Encourage the family to invite everyone to the sacrament – even though the new sign of indifference is for friends to skip "the religious part" and come to the reception (the same is often true of a wedding). The people who do come are often vaguely Catholic or religious; the priest or deacon should give a good short homily or catechesis. Like funerals, it is one of the rare times that the non-church-goer hears the word and can appreciate Catholic liturgy It is one reason I wrote this "charge" or final address to the baptized – to what they are now entitled, and what is the responsibility of this new Christian.

You are now a part of the body of Christ,
a living branch of the vine which is Christ.
You belong to the church, the people of God.
Be faithful, as God is faithful.
You have the right to hear the gospel,
to receive the sacraments,
to have your sins forgiven,
to receive the body and blood of Christ.
You have the calling to live by the gospel,
to be a disciple of Jesus,
loving, serving, forgiving as he did,
believing as he did.

One day reaffirm for yourself
the baptismal vows made for you today
Do not treat lightly or surrender
your inheritance of the Christian faith
and your allegiance to Christ the Lord.

Reconciliation

Yes, we once called it confession. And the sacrament by either name is in considerable disuse and confusion. So theologians and pastors confer, and bishops exhort that we must return to private confession. But listen to this opinion from a rather primary source, the laity. It is a letter in *The Tablet*, England's venerable Catholic weekly, from Philip Binding: "It would save a great deal of time, as well as avoiding incorrect conclusions, if priests made it their business to ask parishioners why they no longer attend the sacrament of reconciliation. They would be told, I am sure, that the problem is a simple one: so many things were defined as sinful without there being a corresponding recognition of their sinfulness in the consciences of the faithful that confession of such 'sins' would not be accompanied by a genuine act of repentance. Participation in a general act of absolution overcomes this hurdle by its very nature and accounts, I suggest, for its growing popularity."

Here is one example of the power of vernacular liturgy - and the Holy Spirit. It was 1969; I began the Mass at St. Paul's Church in Cambridge with the new penitential rite - specifically, the new act of contrition, said by everyone. Is it followed by absolution? It is concluded with the priest's prayer for God to forgive us. It differs from a declaration in the sacrament of penance, "I absolve you." But does anyone really think the entire prayer is not answered, if people say it and mean it, seeking peace and reconciliation? Is the divine mercy limited to the sacraments? No. And we have been chided often by our Orthodox brethren for being too legal in our liturgy, as if we could confine the Holy Spirit. So, does the prayer work? Listen: after the Mass the housekeeper rushed in to confront me: "Did you really mean that prayer you said at the beginning of Mass?" After assuring her I was not on stage, she told me that her daughter, long absent from the sacraments, had been at Mass and told her mother, "That's enough for me!"

Although the confession of sins is omitted from Mass at weddings and funerals, I often use it. The church may be full of people who will be receiving holy communion; they need some kind of spiritual preparation. I use this prayer instead of the alternative, the litany, at every Mass. It is a good prayer, and for the first time we are reminded of sins of omission - asking pardon "for what I have done, and what I have failed to do." And the confession is made "to my brothers and sisters" as well as to almighty God. I have urged sisters and lay ministers in hospitals and on sick calls to use this prayer as a genuine healing of the soul. All honor to the sacrament and the priestly ministry - but we simply can't get around to everyone.

The need continues for moral theologians to rethink our definition of sins. The older categories deal with obedience to law and sins against chastity, personal conduct, and not much more. Sins against neighbor did not seem to include prejudice, racism, and all the various forms of hatred or disdain and social ostracism that have brought so much evil into society. No one seems to recall that to hurl a hateful epithet at a Jew or a Negro (or anyone) was a sin to confess and repent, to do no more. And now we have an awareness of great social problems like pollution, destroying the atmosphere and the future for our children. It is difficult to put this into a personal confession. "Bless me, father, for I have sinned, I kept on using hair sprays that put PCP's into the atmosphere." Or, "I failed to recycle three times." This sounds faintly ridiculous, and it is. A parish committee on social action can focus on these subjects, and they can be reviewed in a service of reconciliation, which would make us aware of our responsibilities.

Indeed such services in parishes, usually in Advent and Lent, have become the most widely used ways of ministering the sacrament of reconciliation. Yes, there is still in particular cases a need for private confession - for instruction, guidance, perhaps for restitution. But there is a greater need to use general absolution. If you wish to hold to the strict view that it should be used only in case of emergency, we are certainly in an emergency right now with the shortage of priests. Pastors and some bishops have recognized for a long time the case for using general absolution. The late bishop of Nashville, Tennessee, Carroll Dozier, who reminded many of Pope John XXIII, gathered his whole flock - or a lot of them - in a large venue for just such a return to grace and the church, giving the forgiveness of sins by general absolution. All this was preceded by intensive preparation in parishes, which were alerted to offer private confession in the following weeks if penitents asked. It was a successful effort until shot down by Rome. The same happened in Australia. And so, the empty confessionals line the old churches, useful for storage. We have much work to do to restore the ministry of God's mercy.

Holy Orders — the Priesthood

The emptying of the seminaries in the western world since the 1960s, only reversed now in a few strongly conservative groups, has led to a crisis we all recognize: aging priests and parishes with no Mass. The emergence of the laity in all branches of parish ministry has been a great gain. But what *is* the specific function of the priest, for what is he ordained? Not primarily to "run parishes" in any material sense; educated parishioners and parish managers, hired or shared or volunteered, are doing that, or should be. Gone is the bishop (we hope) who once bragged to seminarians that "I might not know much theology but I sure know a good piece of real estate when I see it!" Gone is the priest-builder. Collaborator, yes, because he best knows the functions of the building. But the most important thing which he is called to build is the people, the living stones. Gone is the counter of Sunday envelopes, the tallying of donations.

So what do we do? For what are we ordained, called, privileged to do? **To preach the Word. Lead the liturgy. Minister certain sacraments, and oversee the ministry of others. And be a pastor, a leader in the community. A shepherd of the flock, following in the footsteps of Jesus, the Good Shepherd.**

Preaching the word is both demanding and fulfilling. Catholics are catching up with Protestants in preaching the biblical word; we follow a lectionary that major Protestant churches also adopted. But it presents us - indeed, the whole Bible does - with a hugely complicated message that must be winnowed out, explained. The priest doesn't have to be a biblical scholar reading the original languages, but he has to read the commentaries that scholars produce (the ones that are readable). The challenge is to put the text in context, then and now.

Preaching, as anyone knows who has gone from leading a funeral to interpreting Amos on social justice, is both pastoral and prophetic. Not both all the time, but not one all the time. Both roles are challenging in different ways. Pastoral: to give authentic grounds for hope, analogies to human experience as well as the promises of God, and to do this especially while your listeners are confronted with tragic events, personal or social - or just living, trying to live. Wilfred Sheed put it thus: "I have always felt that anyone who has not found the world in some sense a tragic place has just not been paying attention, and anyone who has not adverted to this knowledge within, say, the last three months, has nothing important to tell anyone about anything."

On prophetic preaching: after trying throughout history various economical and social arrangements of money and property, one is still forced to ask, how does one avoid greed and power tearing apart the social fabric and denying to so many a share in God's wealth (the earth) and man's wealth through labor and enterprise? In other words, how do you preach what the Jesuit Walter Burkhardt insistently called "the just word"? And how do you preach any other word? Sometimes the problem is put in that old saying, "Preach truth to power."

Preaching can be and should be shared with the laity, and is now shared with ordained deacons. And the advantage is that often they can put the word in the context of today from their own experience, especially with married life and the working world. One difficulty is that many may not have time to prepare to do at least some exegesis, and to write out a full text; preparing the Sunday homily is not their main preoccupation. But it is, for the priest and the Protestant preacher. This is not an argument for elitism; it is for functionalism, or professionalism. A surgeon or diagnostician trains long years for that interval when you confront him with your problem and await a verdict that may mean life, health, a short life, or death. Seminary training in preaching has been almost uniformly bad (so bad that at one seminary the students formed their own Toastmasters Club to learn to speak on their feet). How do we speak - and what? Biblical studies should continue after the seminary. For how long? Life long. Creative reading and writing has to enter here, more than the standard liberal arts education. Let the communicator learn to write poetry - verse, sonnets, lyrics, the haiku - good essays, even short stories or a play.

There is another aspect of time, or lack of it: the preacher has to engage in reading other fields than scripture. It is revelation with a small "r" that should go on all the time, to illumine and exemplify the biblical insight and the preacher's word. Fiction, poetry, art, films. A good newspaper. Both sides of the conservative and liberal divide. And the scientific journals, at least those one can understand. There are indeed some popularizers of the truths that come from science, authors like Loren Eiseley, Carl Sagan, Jay Gould, and Chet Raymo.

When the Catholic church expands its present small acceptance of married priests, then the preacher with a family will still have to find time. Ask ministers how they proceed; it does become easier. Martin Luther King by the end of his life could build rhetorically and without much of a manuscript, or none at all, on the great themes he knew so well.

The primary charge is the priest as liturgist. The priest at the altar is now called the presider; the word "celebrant" was dropped to emphasize that all the people celebrate. But presider is a weak word, and celebrant is often still in use. Some people joke that the priest should be called "facilitator of charisms." Most of all he leads the celebration of the eucharist. He is indispensable, just as the church is indispensable. The Mass is not his own invention even though it has a wonderful variety to which his own skills can add. The priest is not and never should have been considered to be the magic man or super holy man who "makes Christ come down on earth." *He* does not consecrate the bread and wine, the Holy Spirit does. He lends his voice, hands, body, and presence as the Spirit's instruments; he invokes the Holy Spirit on behalf of the community.

To structure the eucharist effectively, with word, song, gesture, art, and the combined offering of many ministries, is a weekly, even daily, challenge. Time and again people respond to what they call "a good Mass," "a wonderful Mass." They are referring to the role of the priest-presider as well as the music; they appreciate the homily but also the genuineness of someone leading prayer and in communion with God. They understand the experience of being part of a community that welcomes them in this great deed.

There is one other priestly function: it is to be pastor to his people, shepherd of the flock. This takes a lot of living with, loving, sharing. We are, all Christians, called to the ministry of service, compassion, good works. The priest has his own special calling, and it is not diminished by lay ministry. Nothing can diminish it, a sacramental and preaching ministry that gives hope and gladness and meaning to people every day, and on the Sabbath, and at the great transitional moments of life.

The "Circuit Rider Priest"

The shortage of priests has given rise to the "Service of the Word with Holy Communion," conducted by a deacon or a sister, or lay catechist or parish administrator. Holy Communion is given from pre-consecrated hosts kept in the tabernacle. Obviously a priest is needed to renew the supply and to offer Mass, at least occasionally. This situation has deepened the awareness that the parish or local church really is the people, and they take on this responsibility. They certainly can give a homily or read a prepared one. Call it, if you wish, "Today's reflection on the word." This form of Sunday worship - not Mass - is now common in some areas of the United States and has long been common in mission areas where trained lay catechists supply. Liturgical commissions give guidelines and helpful material.

The obvious problem is the lack of the eucharist action. The Mass is not just to receive communion. The substitute service is indeed preferable to closing churches and dispersing parishes, but it is far from ideal to assign the priest to just "drop in" over an ever-widening circuit and liturgical calendar to offer an occasional Mass.

A perceptive letter (*The Tablet*, 4/24/04) from a priest-liturgist protested strongly, and in the name of his brother priests, any arrangement that turned them into "sacrament-dispensing machines." He writes: "Many priests of my acquaintance share the view that we not respond to the Spirit's call to be priests just to celebrate the Mass, we were called to serve the people of God in any way we can, using many and varied talents. This spirituality empowers us not only to help God's people encounter the Paschal Mystery sacramentally but also to experience it in action by our speaking out for the voiceless, being strong for the weak, teaching with conviction and walking in solidarity with the marginalized and oppressed. Indeed, many priests fear a future that would have us defined and limited by sacramental function."

In the past some protested against the inadequate sense of liturgy shown by the so-called hyphenated priests - Jesuits, for example, who were geologists, law professors, economists, administrators, scientists, and specialists of all types. But the liturgical lack has, for the most part, fortunately changed. And there is the argument that they bear extraordinary witness in many fields. Think of Teilhard de Chardin, John Courtney Murray, or the discoverer of the Big Bang Theory, Georges Lemaître, the little-known Belgian priest who earned a doctorate in physics from MIT. To be witnesses for God in so many ways is certainly a vocation for every baptized person but the specialized priest, with his dual role, gives it a special cachet.

Marriage

Yes, it is a sacrament and we should teach this early before the whole concept is lost. Nothing reflects more our secular society than the increasing practice of passing up any kind of church ceremony to locate the whole thing wherever the reception will take place. Or for invited guests to skip "the religious stuff" and go straight to the party. We are not quite in a losing game, but every minister of religion will tell you that weddings are difficult, a challenge to give a sacred dimension to a social event.

Why is it a sacrament (when it was not for so long)? Because the church decided wisely that the love of a man and woman, pledged for life, is a sign of God's love for us. Christ the bridegroom, we the beloved, the bride. Of course - it is a biblical image. Another description came recently from a perceptive person who called it "the sacrament of our sexuality." Never mind how badly the church understood and taught about sexuality in the past; a new day is here when we affirm what we are, what is God-given, and now, should be God-blessed. "Where love is, God is." Why would anyone want to exclude God from the most important act they undertake, made possible by the Creator?

If either or both parties are Catholic, the sacrament should be given as part of a Mass. Dismiss the arguments that it will take too long, is too expensive, etc. The church does allow simply a Service of the Word, but that's a mistake. Look at the symbolic expression of the Mass and how it relates to the two who come before the altar. The Mass is an offering, and they offer themselves to God, to increase the love in the world, and even to create life, as God does. The Mass is a communion, and they seek the most intimate and loving union of all. And in the heart of the Mass the words are spoken which are directly applicable to the man and woman: "This is my body - my life - given for you." Let them give each other communion, and then perhaps assist in giving the sacrament to others.

The Service of the Word is always important, but on this occasion it is probably ineffective; people are not inclined to listen well, and if the readers are chosen from the wedding party (and unrehearsed) the word is not usually proclaimed well. The choice of scriptural readings should go beyond the official listing. The actual Catholic wedding ceremony which takes place after the homily is too short, too legal. As ceremony, liturgy, it needs more expression. Compare it to an Orthodox wedding! If not a crown on the head, perhaps we could be enriched by gestures like a binding of the hands and an embracing of the book of the gospels. I preface the rite with the sublime passage on love from the book of Ruth. And at the end of the nuptial Mass I extend the stole to their shoulders and give them a four-fold blessing (skipping the one prescribed after the Lord's prayer).

The preparation for this sacrament has been richly improved by the required marriage preparation courses, the pre-Cana, even a kind of retreat. The Catholic couple discover to their pleasure that the church considers them the actual ministers of this sacrament, each to the other. None of this richness was present in "the old church" when marriage was strictly viewed as a contractual situation, a legal business.

One Catholic reform has been suggested officially but has not succeeded; it is an alternative beginning of the ceremony to escape the Emily Post etiquette now called "traditional." The new approach suggests that both parents escort their son and daughter in the opening procession. Have done with the old "the father gives away the bride" (the father of the groom is totally ignored the way it is done now). We have not even succeeded in arousing feminists to the fact that the father giving away his daughter is an old feudal custom; she was formerly handed over in exchange for so much property, cattle, land, and then "the bridal" - the bride ale - was drunk to seal the contract. Slowly all this came into the church, where it belongs.

In Germany I saw a wedding that began with everyone gathered outside the church, mingling and enjoying each other. Then the priest and a cross-bearer came out and led the whole crowd in a really joyous procession into the church, with the organ thundering welcome. And yes, this means there are no ushers ostentatiously seating the mothers. The whole surge of people divides by families on either side of the church as they enter. At the end of the procession are the bride and groom and their attendants, who step into the sanctuary. Have you noticed something here - there is no need for a rehearsal!

For the church to discover that marriage should be a sacrament was a great gain. A celebration of human love, of sexuality, in very truth. Of creation: a new family, and very possibly of new life.

CELEBRATING (REALLY) THE LITURGY

Looking Back, and Reclaiming

Look back, if you are old enough, to a few liturgical practices we lost and should reclaim. Like incense. Votive candles. And servers, usually vested. No, not trained by a martinet, and a pox on bishops who are still allowed to ban girl servers. The "in" thing now seems to be to have no servers at all, or adults only, or a family. (But one family "taking over" occasionally as assistants at Mass can indeed be appealing: the parents as lectors and eucharistic ministers, the children welcoming, taking up the collection, bringing up the gifts – as well as serving at the altar.) With young people especially, give them roles to play, and titles, install them with a liturgy. They *can* become reverent and thoughtful. At a funeral the presence of servers with the cross, candles, incense, holy water, and the Book all says something to the people. And the awareness of death might say something to the youngsters.

Use some decent candles. Burn all those tubes with coiled springs inside. Stop thinking how much money is saved by using candle stubs. Or a half-melted paschal candle. Start the fire for all this detritus with the artificial flowers. Haven't people heard of potted plants, ferns, ivy, live and growing things that last for months or all year? One can have a whole tree in the sanctuary or baptistery if a sign of life is wanted. It's not necessary to have expensive cut flowers all year long. Bring them in from the fields if possible. (Has anyone replaced holy water fonts with a flowing fountain?)

When Passiontide was shrunk to Holy Week some change was needed but who decided it was no longer the thing to veil the statues in purple? In the old days we had a visual effect in all our churches that struck everyone. I know there were some pious explanations about the saints veiling their faces, horror-stricken at what we did to Jesus. The point is that you didn't need any explanation at all - the whole tone of the church was different; it "got to you." The purple cloth was a shroud; the bride was in mourning. If there are no statues, drape the church itself (as is often done in Rome). And it was a big deal to remove all this at the Gloria on Holy Saturday morning while the servers banged away nonstop with the bells. Of stuff like this are children's memories made. What do they remember now?

Holy Saturday was turned back to the Easter Vigil - at last. But whatever happened to blessing the bread and taking home the holy water? The Poles would never let you get away without blessing the bread. And Greeks even bring home the Easter fire.

Some practices should not return, like dressing up kids like little cardinals for Corpus Christi processions. But people still like special clothes, parades, carnivals, a kaleidoscope, some color and solemnity. We used to get this, with a degree of religious sensitivity, in church. It was not all pomp and circumstance; it fulfilled a human need.

Sundays and Holy Days

Many things keep us from being a joyful people. Temperaments. Bad weather! And the latent, just waiting tragic trip-ups of life. There is a further reason which is cultural, and it impoverishes western industrial societies, particularly in the United States. Put simply, we don't know how to be joyful, to rejoice; we have lost the skills. Consider that when we meet socially, we do three things: eat, drink, and talk. Wonderful, but each has limitations! So what else could we do? *Sing. Dance. And play.* But these are the skills - the joy of living and enjoying each other - which we have forgotten. On my campus a student passes, walking quickly. She is listening to her iPod. Her cell phone rings. Both ears are engaged. And she is on her way to the café to unfold her laptop. So we are wired for sound. And what else?

There is a line from the psalms, "I rejoiced when they said to me, let us go up to the house of the Lord!" It is not likely that those who go to Sunday Mass feel that exuberant about it. Children might, if they are going to have some role, like singing, serving, acting out the gospel. In earlier times people went because "they had to" - that is, it was a strict church law to attend Mass on Sundays and holy days, and the dread phrase followed, "under pain of mortal sin."

But there were other motives. Before World War II there was not much else to do on Sunday. No shopping, no malls, no athletic contests. No television, no wireless world. And there was a deeper reason they came and filled the great churches, now largely empty or sold, demolished, or combined with other parishes. It was *right* to go to church, to Mass. The obligation of church law was not as deep as the obligation of the creature to acknowledge the Creator. To worship. They would not put it in those terms but they felt or intuited it. There is a passage in Thomas Merton's autobiography, *Seven Story Mountain,* which occurs before his famed conversion and the life and writing that led so many more to holiness and God. Very much a secular and dissolute youth, he was staying briefly with a French peasant family; he observed their piety, their faithfulness in going to Mass, their obvious belief in God. An atmosphere of faith. When he tried to give an alternative explanation for life - for everything - they simply said, "It is not possible." They could not explain further; try as well to explain why you love your family.

Creatures should bow down (or fall down) before their Creator; children should acknowledge their Parent God. The church law seeks to express this as an obligation to worship. *But change the emphasis from obligation to celebration, and make it so expressive in ritual, song, music, inclusiveness and participation, that people will be eager to come, crowd in, be glad to be part of the worship community.*

A Broadway play some years ago had a wonderful title: "Your Arms Are Too Short to Box with God." As the chorus dances out for a rip-roaring Sunday service (in good Baptist or evangelical style) the refrain, repeated with enormous enthusiasm, is "We're gonna have a good time!" Do you think a congregation, old or young, would say that about the average Sunday worship? And can you do this without abandoning all "tone," or the right kind of propriety?

Harvey Cox, the long-time professor of religion at Harvard University, has pointed out that the church has been called to do four things in connection with the good news: to *proclaim* it, to *witness* it (by its lifestyle and its people), to *affirm* it (by which he means to support anyone who advances the kingdom of God – a really powerful suggestion), and one more - to *celebrate* it. We haven't made a good transition from obligation to celebration. And yet we have known all along that great doctrines like Incarnation and Resurrection are conveyed for the most part by the liturgical year and the way we celebrate, the rituals and symbols we use. To repeat, we really don't have enough of the arts of celebration, including dance, processions, banners, a colorful use of cloth, song and music. The same Harvey Cox observed that it really is strange that the Catholic church which, like all Christian churches, rises up from the great event of resurrection and new life, then proceeds to clothe its professional people in funereal black. But at least that's not true at the eucharist. And that is a sign that we should do much more.

Think about our holy days. Some urge dropping them altogether because they inconveniently occur often on a weekday. Or combine them with Sundays, which sometimes means displacing the regular liturgy. **A better solution would be to celebrate holydays with one great evening Mass.** A Marian festival - or a celebration of Jesus' Ascension. Or All Saints. Or the patron saint or feast of the parish. Just one Mass; pour everything into one great hour (with fun and food afterwards). Combine the choirs. Bring on - spend money - a soloist or great violinist or flutist whose artistry will thrill the soul. Let the trumpets sound. Forget all the old rules about obligation (two generations now neither advert or even know them). If you have a real celebration, with excellent preaching and music, with colorful banners, perhaps with liturgical dance and processions and joyous song - a real festivity - the crowds will come. This approach is far better than removing special days altogether from the calendar and losing more of our Catholic identity.

Is all this feasible or just theory? No; I've seen it done, at least with occasional Sunday Masses. I think back on the artistry of a choir and their leader at Saint Ignatius Church adjoining the Boston College campus. People joined the choir because she made them sing so well, and she communicated a real *joie de vivre.* Her name, appropriately, was the Latin word for rejoicing, Laetitia (Blaine). The liturgical year would unfold with a repertoire of good hymns and Mass propers but also with surprises - such as the Sunday before the holiday for Martin Luther King. It became customary, after one glorious performance, to end that Mass each year with the Negro spiritual, "Lights of the City." It builds to a crescendo, and takes eight minutes. Now this is a congregation with a complete range of professors and porters, Asian, Latin, black, Italian, Irish new and old, the majority professionals who do not usually sing negro spirituals. They sang this one; most of them even rocked with it. And occasionally at a funeral, they sang another spiritual, "We Shall Meet by the Waters." An eclectic program? Yes.

Celebrations can also be for the great transitus from death to life - eternal life. I think of another parish in my Kansas days, the funeral of a young priest who had been tragically killed. The grief was huge. So was the song as they bore his coffin from the church. It filled the air, the whole church still singing the Deiss arrangement of "My Shepherd is the Lord." The funeral of the beloved Cardinal Bernardin in Chicago should be studied for many things to emulate. The congregation sang over and over that plaintive melody from Taizé, the single line, "Jesus, remember me when you come into your kingdom." And, for me, another unforgettable liturgy: on that terrible day of 9/11, five thousand students at a Mass that evening in the Boston College arena, singing, in tears and hands joined, the song from the Saint Louis Jesuits, *Be Not Afraid,* with the piercing verse: "If you pass through raging waters you shall not be drowned. If you walk amid the burning flames, you shall not be harmed. If you stand before the pow'r of hell and death is at your side, know that I am with you through it all." The terrible images of death that day were suddenly put in the context of salvation, in the hands of the One who saves.

Some music directors will object to the quality of this or that composition. Some do not like, for instance, the range of that other most used hymn at funerals, Sister Suzanne Toolan's "I will raise him up on the last day." Or the number one favorite, "On Eagles' Wings." But participation and "the people's liturgy" count heavily here.

The use of banners exploded in some places with "the new Mass." Formerly they were mostly used to identify pious fraternities. Now they richly express the liturgical year. As tapestries they can decorate the church, even in monumental style; the new cathedral in Los Angeles is a stunning example. Banner makers in a parish can profit from much how-to literature. In Detroit I found this art so well developed with rather expensive and beautifully made banners that the parishes instituted a "swap around" program to share the talents.

The Place for Dance

The pastor of St. Ignatius church in Newton, Massachusetts, Father Robert VerEecke, S.J., whose parents were both opera singers, is so skilled with ballet and interpretative dance that his creation and choreography of "A Dancer's Christmas" has become over twenty-five years an esteemed part of the Christmas canon in Boston. He favors an occasional use of dance in the liturgy, and writing in *America* magazine (3/25/02) he mentions the various criticisms or prohibitions that have come from authority (despite the fact that dancers more than once have participated in papal liturgy). He is committed to carrying out the injunction of the psalmist "to praise God's name in the festive dance" (Ps. 149). And another psalm (150) calls on us to "praise God with timbrel and dance." All this he rightly calls *embodied prayer,* and says, "Doesn't the resurrection of Jesus make us want to jump for joy and leap for love?" My own sense is that too often we are a joyless people who have lost the gifts of folk dance and group singing. They can be reclaimed. That Shaker hymn we all sing, or should, calls Jesus "the Lord of the Dance," and tells us to "dance, dance, wherever you may be." Then let's do it or learn how. Think of traditional folk dances - Hebrew, Greek, Russian, and other cultures - with everybody involved at weddings. The inclusion of the dance in the Mass is rare in the west. When done, as in an offertory procession, would it be acceptable? To most people, yes. Think how many children learn ballet. It is difficult to imagine parents being upset at children gracefully presenting the gifts at Mass - the most obvious time. Otherwise the ritual does not have much room, but it is different at Holy Week liturgies and in gathering for prayer. Embodied prayer.

One more VerEecke touch at St. Ignatius: while many have used mime or ballet to present the story of the passion as read on Palm Sunday, his approach with cloth has great impact. The dancers first unfold a long red cloth on the sanctuary floor, making it the Last Supper table around which the disciples and Jesus gather. And they did. As the narration continues, they wrap the cloth around Jesus; it is now the garment with which Herod's soldiers clothed him, to mock his kingship. Then, held out horizontally with Jesus' arms entwined, it is the arm of the cross. And when the dread story is ended, the Dancers take the cloth once more and now it becomes the altar cloth for the Mass - which always celebrates his victory over sin and death.

We used to say that the red print in the liturgical books are the rubrics, the black print is the liturgy. The black print, of course, includes all the scriptures, the prayers, the proclamation and acclamations, and this is the word that takes flesh in us. We are reminded that the Latin rite in the west is traditionally sober, and dancing is not easily accepted in church by many. But we are still embodied creatures. Could we not learn from others, and be enriched? I think of being in Barcelona, Spain, sharing the eleven o'clock Mass at the cathedral. The people leave afterwards and join others with the musicians in the square to dance the Sardana, the traditional Catalan folk dance forbidden under the Franco oppression. It is a joyous scene. There were two large circles, one of older people, the other very youthful. Can you imagine your parishioners leaving the church after Sunday Mass and dancing in the square?

Easter On

The readings of the Mass for Easter Sunday cry out for a dramatic presentation and rearrangement of the Service of the Word. Do it and see how "reading" can turn into proclamation, how narration can become Good News. But first you have to get out of the pews all copies of the scripture (the missalettes) for at least today's worship. Make up your own "order of worship," without the readings.

The first reading is from Peter; it is a sermon - the original sermon, the *kerygma.* Save it. One passage from Paul (*I Corinthians 5: 6-8*) is a call to worship: "Come, let us celebrate the feast, not with the old yeast, but with the unleavened bread of sincerity and truth!" Why delay this "call to worship" until well after the celebration has begun? Paul's words are an echo of John's gospel, "The time is coming, indeed is now here, when those who worship the Father must worship him in Spirit and in truth." Begin the Mass with Paul's exhortation. Let it ring out, and follow with song (or the Easter sequence). Or a great ringing of the bells at the Gloria. People might be encouraged (especially children) to bring their own bells.

The gospel deserves Alleluias, of course, and flourishes and trumpets, and perhaps a great hymn afterwards. And a better gospel choice than one that just presents us with the empty tomb. At least extend the passage from John to the meeting of

Christ with Magdalen. As for the first reading, it would make a good final summary after communion of all that God has done and we have celebrated on this first of days. But there is much more to do with the Easter liturgy - the whole of Easter.

For many years since the first and greatest celebration of Easter was returned to the evening hours (the Easter Vigil) we extolled this great liturgy of light and darkness, baptismal renewal, great music (including the famous deacon's hymn, the *Exsultet,* to the light of Christ symbolized by the paschal candle). And it works - except for the fact that the greater crowd by far jams the churches on Easter *morning,* not the night before. It seemed to me long ago that we should repeat some of the Easter symbolism at each Mass, such as the renewal of baptismal vows, the asperges, even the sharing of the light from the Christ candle. Gradually, all those elements have been incorporated indeed with each Easter Mass.

And then? Easter stops. No one has expressed this better than an Anglican pastor, Father Andrew Walker, who tells of a standard conversation on Monday or Tuesday after the famous feast. Parishioner: "Did you have a good Easter, Vicar!" He observes that no one greets him one or two days after Ash Wednesday and asks, "Did you have a good Lent, Vicar!" They *know* Lent goes on for six weeks. And so, we have a problem. Is it impossible to get across the understanding that Easter is even more important than Lent, and continues in the liturgical calendar for seven weeks, not six, and climaxes in the last, best gift of God, the Holy Spirit, to continue making us an Easter people in the world?

Walker made his own contribution with a graceful book that he calls *Journey into Joy.* Its subtitle is "Stations of the Resurrection." And he presents the events of Christ's risen life for our meditation, aided by an excellent choice of prayer, poetry, and art.

But the problem continues: what to do with the seven weeks of Easter in our churches? I would argue that all the gospel accounts of the encounters with the Risen Christ should be read, and certainly the one that governs all others, the foundational statement of the early church's belief in resurrection, Paul's *I Corinthians 11.* Celebrate (as is often done) the first Holy Communions and, if possible, the Confirmations in the Easter season. Invite those newly baptized at the Easter Vigil to a parish supper, and perhaps introduce them at one of the Masses in Eastertide. I have also given at this time (or really anytime) a series of lectures on eschatology and building a resurrection faith; it is so fundamental to who we are and how we live with hope.

Experimental Liturgies

There are three approaches to adaptation of the liturgy. One is rigidly structured, strictly according to the book, ignoring even the considerable latitude which is now official. These people are afraid of change, afraid of any personalism, even afraid of silence, such as the rubrics now recommend after the communion. 'Busyprayer'. There is another group which improvises with what they call Mass all the way. All they need is "a loaf of bread, a jug of wine, and thou." They are borrowing from a tradition which they often refuse to recognize or help. And then there is the third group which uses formal tradition with a certain style and spirit. They are adaptable, creative, pastoral, yes, and authentically human.

At the height of experimental liturgies I was urged to visit a parish in San Diego: it was (perhaps still is) poor, black, and integrated by visitors and adopted parishioners. I was told it had "spirit" and "community," but the Rotary and the pep squad have those, too. So I went with two friends to see "the body," and find out what form the Incarnation takes. We were warned to come early and prepare to stay late. Obligations can wrap up in 20 minutes; celebrations and love affairs don't steal a look at watches.

It was hard to tell where the pews stopped and the people started. We wound up in the front pew; in this church the front was the middle; they spilled over into chairs and every spare corner of the sanctuary. The altar rail seated small children nicely - you can't swing your legs in an ordinary pew. The music came from a group called with affection "our orchestra." Two electronic guitars, a banjo, two drummers, a girl with tambourines, and another with maracas. One drummer was an eleven-year-old Negro boy, poised and serious. Too serious, I thought, until his face lit up when I sought out the musicians to congratulate them. The other drummer was blind. He came in with his wife; he was a strong young man whose hands moved with utter fluidity over the two long, oval drums while his head moved in a constant figure-eight pattern, a perfect synchronization. He told me, "I'm a professional musician, and I've been to lots of Masses; but I just never thought I'd be playing my skins here."

The pastor said the musicians invite their friends and this was wonderful as well as unpredictable; the music succeeded because they were fine musicians, and the beat was irresistible. The music-makers were a sign of contemporary community: four white, two black; every age, income, and style of dress. They were not a boys' choir: uniform, hand-screened, cherubic. The latter is a sign of selectivity; here the principle was inclusive, suggesting that making music and, ultimately, making gladness, joyful living, belong to everyone; the whole community contributes and creates: those who couldn't play, sang; and those who couldn't sing certainly got in on the rhythm. Children dance at these Masses; they can't help it. In other churches they sit in proper silence (except to ask, "When can we go home?").

After rehearsals Mass began with "The King of Glory" hymn. It is one of the best (Father Willard Jabusch), and a song for tambourines and drums. It began slowly but the tempo and the beat increased, and the chorus built up like waves pounding on the shore. What really took place was an expansion of consciousness: "The King of glory comes, the nation rejoices; open the gates before Him, *lift up your voices*!"

The feast and theme of "family" were announced; then a new *Kyrie* began. It was done by "lining," a method from the frontier and preliterate days for teaching a hymn painlessly, sans books, sans practice. You just follow a good vocalist, line by line. And so we did. The music rose, fell, died, surged again, pleaded with the Lord of mercy, and calmed down to a serene sense of trust. The *Gloria* was the traditional text, sung very fully.

The Epistle was read by another blind man, who came to the lectern with his wife, unfolded his large Braille book, and changed the atmosphere immediately with his powerful reading. The pastor made a strong pitch for the symbolism of the gifts. "The bread and wine are *you*," he said, "and if not, bringing them up is an empty gesture." The *Sanctus* and the *Agnus Dei* were high points of the music; Sister Miriam Therese of the Medical Mission Sisters, who wrote "Spirit of God," would have been elated.

After the beginning of a brief canon, everyone, to my surprise, picked up with the words of institution: "On the night before he died...." I didn't agree, but this had a strange power as the whole church said: "This is my body, which will be given up for you." The eternal has no boundaries, and it is by the internal process of knowing love and loving knowledge that we remove our own boundaries. But the way is, inevitably and rather wonderfully, in and through the body. So what all these people were saying in that parish was not merely, "This is my body," but "This is *me*, the whole of me. And I give myself to you, holding nothing back. My gift is not just verbal; I'll put my body on the line. I'll use myself up, wear myself out, run myself down. And I will reach out, lift up, help someone who's down. I won't do this alone. The Christ-in-me will do it."

And more: "The one beside me, who is saying the same words, is 'me' also. We are all *in* this one body, which is the new way your Son lives among us. It is a beautiful body - black, white, old, young, strong, feeble; tumbling blond hair, sightless eyes and twisted limbs, dancing feet and swinging children's legs - it's all this body of Christ which we are struggling, Lord, to give to you or use in your service."

It's people who matter, so I tried to focus on a few. One was a four-year-old girl, swinging from her perch on the altar rail, who suddenly came down and stood beside the blind lector to look at his praying hands as they moved over the Braille. She was motionless for the entire six minutes. Then there was the blond server with the fall of long, brushed hair; his white alb was well styled, and full length, but it didn't quite conceal his tooled leather boots. He had none of the drummer boy's intensity but his body moved constantly with the rhythms that came so insistently through the Mass. He was listening with his body, responding to the music, just as the young drummer was caught up by his artistry, and the little girl by the absorbing performance of the blind reader. Our usual involvement in Mass is static, formal, linear. One reads or speaks a fixed line; the words come half-alive but die quickly. Here the participation is many-layered, and has picked up the rhythms and variety of human life. The children were not disorderly because the older order had never been imposed, and there were moments when they moved into rapt attention.

The priest came through as a loving human being. Vested, of course - not that he was a better man; he was the lead man. And his vestment was a signal, like the flag that starts the auto races, a sign that said something wonderful and mysterious is going to happen in this hour, something that means there is hope - hope that our happiness might make it all the way. His chasuble was made of red, black, and white squares, in African-style.

Was it a sense of joy that predominated? Yes, but more one of acceptance, belonging, and a certain readiness to talk, relax, and share. There were times when you were invited to talk with your neighbor, and a mother with her 15-year-old son told me she came here every Sunday because she felt so welcome. "Enjoy, enjoy!" (as Harry Golden's Jewish mother used to say) was close to their spirit. So much music and delight in religion make people think it *must* be wrong. We may be made for joy, but we don't want to admit it or act like it (in most other parishes). Is all this "new worship" an emotional binge, something the Pentecostals do better?

No. Even with all this acoustic overlay, there was a significant continuity established by the eucharistic symbols of book and bread and wine. There was also an altar, cross, candles, and vestments; these were identity points. When a rite is enlivened with a genuine spirit - and I am speaking of the one Spirit who is Holy - and this is done in a eucharistic setting, with the remembered but not slavish traditions of the Catholic Mass, you have both tradition and creativity. You are going somewhere, not pausing for fifteen minutes of effusion by someone who's "got Jesus." We all need to "get him," to sense his Spirit as an impetus to live, live better, and love more. But this power is realized and communicated in sounds which are more specific than music - with words, and with object-rites which are more than audible - the gifts, the offering, the Communion, the embracing, blessing, taking hands.

In any good Sunday celebration both speech and music are used, and each is sound conveying meaning. The sound of music is more exalting and transforming. But the words give it a boundary, not to fence it in but to establish the link with here and now, with reality. Music is like the link to Spirit, and speech to the Logos. Music lifts one to the heights, and all the other rites - as homely as eating a meal or shaking hands - make sure you are not floating away, that you still wear the flesh and walk the good earth God has made.

There was nothing unusual about the church building. The tired old style of poor stained glass was there, and plaster stations of the cross, etc. But if the art was stereotyped, the sound was stereo. A few banners changed the appearance slightly, but not on a monumental scale. In some atmospheres (the campus, or a new-breed parish) I would not be at ease with the left-over "art." But here there was a comfortable feeling of old and new. It was good to see what could be done just with people. The new wine had really burst the old bottles and created a new spirit. Older people found here some points of reference, and a new generation had no hang-ups; for them "it's a brand-new day."

Finding the Balance

Annie Dillard, the essayist who wrote *Pilgrim at Tinker's Creek* and *Teaching a Stone to Talk,* tells in the latter volume of her experience of Mass in a way that may help one to find the balance between popular liturgy (a so-called folk Mass) and the beauty of a sung Mass offered by people who take (decidedly) a more classical route. She took a long road into Catholicism and on the way describes with a certain horror her first encounter of a guitar group at Mass. They were called the Wildflowers, really Californian, colorfully assorted and attired. When the Sanctus (Holy, Holy, Holy) part of the Mass arrives, it is for her a contemplative prayer but not today – a sudden riff on the guitar announces a pop version: "Heaven and earth / (Heaven and earth earth earth earth earth) / Are full (full full full) / Of your glory..." Does she flee to high liturgy or a more refined Episcopalian service? No, one of the reasons she sought out Catholicism is that she found it really catholic, a gathering of all sorts of people. Yes, seeking God. Or meaning to life. Or how to get through life. She writes of the elderly priest reading, in a fatherly way, the petitions asking desperately for prayer, and thinks that the sound of his creaking knees as he genuflects is a lovely music. Her passage on worship as self abasement before the Creator exaggerates a little! But to read it makes one wonder if we need ways to show a deeper reverence before the mystery of God:

> **Does anyone have the foggiest idea what sort of power we so blithely invoke? Or, as I suspect, does no one believe a word of it? The churches are children playing on the floor with their chemistry sets, mixing up a batch of TNT to kill a Sunday morning. It is madness to wear ladies' straw hats and velvet hats to church; we should all be wearing crash helmets. Ushers should issue life preservers and signal flares; they should lash us to our pews.**

Then the book adopts a surreal style; she combines her venture into Mass with the tale of the English explorers seeking the North Pole. That story is a true and absurdly tragic account. They all die seeking "the true north" which is obviously a metaphor for seeking God. But now, in a flight of fancy, she puts all the Wildflowers and the priest with the creaking knees and Oswald the newborn baby and the English explorers on an ice cap that moves closer to the goal.

Matter and Form

One cannot do anything and call it Mass. There is a "matter and form" for each sacrament to keep it from being formless or invalid (and in some cases, bizarre). We don't baptize with any prayer we wish but in the name and the power of the Father, Son, and Holy Spirit. When a priest overly concerned about sexism in the liturgy changed the formula to "In the name of the Creator, Redeemer, and Sanctifier," all his baptisms were ruled invalid by the bishop, which struck some as an equal over-reaction. But when I recently baptized Jonathan in the name of the Trinity, he was a vigorous 14-month-old, strong enough to roll over completely just as I finished "in the name of the Son." We had to roll him back for the Holy Spirit! I wrote him about it later; someday he can learn that he really is a temple of the Holy Spirit, to use Paul's words, and call upon this "divine energy," wisdom and enlightenment when he needs help to live his life and be a Christian.

But speaking of validity, why does the church insist with the eucharist on using two foods, bread and wine, which are not common for many peoples who eat rice or beans or maize or something else each day? Or drink sake instead of wine? Some object further that the sign value here is not the object but the action: breaking and sharing food and drink. True enough, but we use approximately what Jesus used at the Last Supper to anchor this event in an historic reality. Christianity is a happening, not just a philosophy. It is in the world, part of the world, and intended to change the world. True enough, but some modification of bread and wine is or should be allowed.

Creative Tension

In the 1960s the Liturgical Conference sought a greater outreach to other Christian faiths and a more experimental form of worship; this resulted in lively and inclusive liturgies at the annual Liturgical Weeks, but also some protests. This is understandable. Imagine going from a monastic style liturgy with Gregorian chant or the elaborate style (still) at the Brompton Oratory in London to encounter what some describe as a "hootenanny Mass." I have been deafened by a smash-banging "people's Mass" and also bemused by the long, drawn out singing of the creed at a very formal church. But I have shared my feeling for the great classical music at Masses in Germany which blend in vernacular prayer and hymns. Once I offered Mass on a mountaintop with an outcropping of rock for an altar. "Rock of ages." It was there when Jesus was born. All we brought were bread and wine and a gospel. The rising sun was our light, and silence the music.

There is a solution for the occasional conflict. Experimental liturgies should be the approved work of liturgical study centers at our universities. But creativity should be accepted in parish liturgies. And also with youth groups; the German hierarchy recently suggested that special churches be designated for youth to celebrate Mass in their own style. In all this, there will always be a tension between form and freedom. It should be a creative tension.

Devotions and Liturgy

For the longest time, during the eclipse of liturgical prayer or popular participation in the Mass, devotions were the principal way that people prayed. And all prayer is good; there is need for understanding here, not opposition. But also a need to find the right balance. For instance, the old and favorite place to pray the rosary in public was at Mass. After all, when else did Catholics gather? It was an unenviable spectacle of the priest doing his thing at the altar and the people doing theirs in the pews, pausing only in the Hail Marys for the consecration, and finishing the rosary by the communion. As for devotion to the Blessed Sacrament, it was often confused or combined with what was going on at the altar. The monstrance is an elaborate vessel to contain and display the consecrated host; in a practice no longer allowed it was sometimes placed on the altar or above it while the Mass was going on. Double genuflections were required. Since there were no public prayers at Mass for people's needs, they were, at pastoral whim, just added on: five Hail Marys for rain. Or, to stop raining. Personal petitions, usually heartfelt pleas for healing, sometimes for finding a job or to save a marriage, were incorporated into novenas.

And there have been many such devotions; the novena to the Sorrowful Mother drew such large crowds in Chicago that traffic control was necessary. In Jesuit churches it has been the novena to St. Francis Xavier; elsewhere, the Miraculous Medal, from a vision to St. Catherine Laboure. And a private revelation from Saint Margaret Mary resulted in the devout practice of going to Mass and receiving Holy Communion on nine consecutive first Fridays. The promise was that one would thereby be sure to die in the state of grace and thus enter heaven. This kind of approach is less than desirable, and led to questions such as, "What if I miss one Friday? Can I make it up?" An old joke (perhaps true) is told of the wife who lit all the candles before St. Joseph's statue to gain his intercession for her husband seeking a job. When he didn't get the job she returned to blow them all out, retorting "You're a fine friend of the workingman!" Another practice which is no joke and still going on, is to enlist St Joseph's help in selling a house. You bury his statue - upside down, and wait for the customers. Special small statues are even sold for that purpose. These pious horrors are not imagined - you may remember the claim a few years ago that Mother Teresa's image appeared on a cinnamon bun.

The number nine - nine consecutive days or times of prayer - probably came from the nine days which the liturgical calendar gives from the Feast of the Ascension to Pentecost; the scripture describes the disciples and Mary constant in prayer, and the answer was the sublime gift of the Holy Spirit. Numbers are useful in setting a pattern but they can easily become superstitious. Is a "four-way medal" better than one? Is lighting just one candle - a votive light - sufficient? In the redecoration of churches, some removed the votive candles completely or replaced them with the hideous efficiency of small light fixtures turned on a by a coin. It was a mistake. Lighting a candle is a universal symbol.

Where was preaching in all this? Often it took place during novenas, and always in parish retreats or missions. That is another story. Those were the days when men were separated from women for separate mission sermons. The emphasis was usually on a making a good confession and staying out of hell. Wives were reminded they had a duty to "submit to their husbands" and that often meant a new crop of babies nine months later. As for hellfire preaching, you still find people who admire or wish it back. Their penance should be to read the account by James Joyce in *The Diary of the Artist as a Young Man* of just such a mission sermon (preached by a Redemptorist, not a Jesuit, as the book incorrectly says), and which helped lead to Joyce's disavowal of Catholicism.

The devotional life is a special richness of the Catholic tradition. Think of the Marian shrines, the extraordinary devotion over a century and a half at Lourdes in France, of the Mexican people to Guadalupe, the devotion of Pope John Paul II and so many more to Fatima, the multiple street processions and pious societies in Holy Week, especially in Spain, the statues crowned and carried through the streets in so many places, especially in Italy and the "little Italys" of the United States. And then there are the blessings of just about everything – houses, automobiles, boats, the fishing fleet, pets, rosaries, medals and so on. These are sacramentals and an official part of liturgy but a caution or correction is needed here. One does not just sprinkle holy water on automobiles, or anything else, without at least a few words to keep it from a superstitious act. There certainly is no guarantee that this blessing or St. Christopher's medal means you will never have an accident. What it does mean, I suggest, is that you drive with care for others and perhaps find ways to share the vehicle, especially with the house-ridden and the poor. And so it can indeed be a gracious act. The same with the popular ritual of blessing the throats by touching the candles to them on the Feast of St. Blase. Of course we may pray for help or cure, but also, may we speak words of compassion and truth.

Of all the sacramentals the use of ashes on Ash Wednesday is by far the most sought after (palms on Palm Sunday are second). Churches are crowded on Ash Wednesday with many people we don't see again until Easter. Fr. Godfrey Diekmann liked to tell of assisting at a church in Mexico on Palm Sunday and being told by the pastor that the palms would be blessed and given out after the Mass, not before. The Benedictine pointed out the obvious, that the ceremony was prescribed for the beginning, to set the tone for the liturgy and for the people to hold the palms during the procession and reading of the Passion. No matter; the pastor said that if you give them out before, they would skip the Mass!

For many people, devotions are the only or major link with the faith. And it fulfills an obvious need; with a billion or more Christians there will always be a variety of ways to pray. And the church needs to provide those sacred objects - the cross or crucifix above all, the pictures and statues, rosaries and medals that are "holy reminders." A devotion to the Sacred Heart is a concrete way to express the most fundamental truth that God is love. It deserves good art. It is the mind of the church that devotions should be inspired by the liturgy and lead to a greater appreciation of it. We have gained from studying and emulating the Orthodox approach to icons. The sacred image in their tradition invites to contemplation, to "go through" the image to the reality. And iconography continues as a great art.

But it is difficult to curb excesses or a sense of magic. Think of the *flagellantes*, the masochistic practices which the church tries to eliminate or condemn. And all of those absurdly reported images of Mary or Jesus appearing on bank windows or just about anywhere. The bleeding crosses. The sun rotating in the heavens. The rosaries supposedly turned to gold. The poor, ill, or dying people whom the gullible consider to be seers or mystics and the source of miracles. And not least, the exploitation of ill people supposedly possessed by the devil. It was a scandal for a bishop to allow an exorcism to become a spectacle on television. No one denies evil; it just isn't cast out this way.

The devotion to Mary can have much more liturgical expression than is now given. For example, Vespers (or Evensong) concludes with the Magnificat, Mary's song in Luke's gospel. The solemn chant melody is appealing. There are five Marian anthems or hymns for Vespers that are used, at least in monasteries, during the church year; we know only one, the Salve Regina (Hail Holy Queen). They are simple chants that could easily become common prayer. The praying of the Angelus could be revived. If one really wishes to see Marian piety and great poetry expressed in the liturgy, find and pray the Akathistos ("standing up") Hymn. It is prayed as a Vesper service in the Byzantine rite, both east and west. The metaphors for the Mother of God and the miracle of the Incarnation and the gospel episodes of her life are like precious jewels, high poetry, far beyond anything we use in the Latin rite.

CRITIQUES OF LITURGICAL REFORM

Loss of the Sacred?

To start a discussion, read the chapter on the eucharist in the recent book, *Faith of Our Fathers,* by Eamon Duffy. He asks if we did not abandon too much of the mystical or symbolic element in moving from the Mass of Paul V (often called, incorrectly, the Tridentine Mass) to the reformed rite of Paul VI which we celebrate today. It is not just a matter of restoring, if we should, incense and bells, kneeling and genuflections; it is really a question of eucharistic theology. Or, to put it too simply, the dual understanding of the body of Christ: the consecrated host and the consecrated people. The first phrase we recognize as the center of eucharistic devotion; the second, as the primary purpose and original intent of "doing Mass." Read again the simple description of the eucharist from Justin Martyr. Go deeply, and read the anaphora (eucharistic prayer) from St. Basil. Then read any book on liturgical history that shows the development of pontifical and high court liturgy, a truly baroque style that increasingly made the people spectators who were motivated to "see the host" – and adore it – but not to receive it.

If one is up to reading a saga and a great, even famous novel, *Kristin Lavransdatter,* by Sigrid Undset, it presents more than one description of what it meant to go to Mass in thirteenth century Norway. Faith and devotion were certainly evident, but a very different style of prayer or participation.

Read the papal documents that over several decades called for restoring "full and active participation in the sacred liturgy as the primary and indispensable source of the Christian spirit." What has been the result? The reform of the whole liturgy, which includes the Divine Office, the sacraments, the church year, and the sacramentals. But especially it means the Mass we have today, which certainly fits that phrase, "a work in progress." Much has been achieved. The weekend Mass is a gracious hour, not a rushed half hour. And no longer "on the hour, every hour." Lay people are visible and audible in various roles which reflect - and we must deepen this understanding - their share in Christ's priesthood. This is still not understood but held in suspicion, as if becoming a eucharistic minister (or even preparing and cleansing the communion vessels) is something that should be returned to the sacred hands of the priest. This is wildly illogical; if lay assistants are worthy to handle and distribute the host with their hands, surely they may cleanse the vessels used. And this should happen in the sacristy, to facilitate the end of the Communion rite (and the time for silence and thanksgiving). The old school loves to stress that the authorization for eucharistic ministers, a truly significant change, specifically calls them "extraordinary ministers," thus emphasizing the priest as the ordinary or usual one. This has resulted in some angry situations like a parish confirmation, with priests in attendance, where lay ministers were denied their role. When the lay role was introduced, one heard of people, not all old, who would refuse to receive the host from a lay person, and especially if it was a woman. Cross over to the line where a priest distributed communion? This happened.

We need a better and more patient explanation on two levels of the eucharistic ministry. The first is pragmatic: the scarcity of priests. And the new number of communicants. The ability now to reach more often those confined by illness and age; to send forth the eucharistic messenger was indeed the practice of the early church. But then, as the novel we mentioned illustrated, the host was carried by a priest, close to his heart, and he was preceded by a server, both of them in full holy attire. The server would ring a bell or carry a candle. This was especially true in earlier societies, in rural villages - where most of us do not live now! But what of courtesy, piety, our ritual procedures? Has all this become too casual? In Catholic homes is the customary (in the old days) sick call set - holy water, candle, and linen cloth - still in use? Eamon Duffy in the text cited gives us observations of the utterly careless way of children receiving communion. Drilled and pious for the first communion, yes. But afterwards? A formal piety that included kneeling, silence, and prayer is largely gone. Is it adequate to replace it with a communion hymn? The hymn is intended to unite us as a community. The other approach stresses solitary piety, the individual before God.

There are arguments for both sides; a discussion might be guided by these points:

1. Any major change in habitual ways of doing things, especially sacred rituals, involves upset; something indeed is lost, the familiar, and the meaning this conveyed. But are there commensurate gains? The return to the vernacular language is a case in point, as we have noted. Many, although a minority, loved the Latin, but it was used scarcely more than Esperanto as a world language; in short, it was not the vernacular. And now the people hear. And read; to print the words of the Mass is no longer forbidden. Lay missals were often restricted in the past.

2. In attempting to achieve what Duffy describes well as the community aspect of the eucharist - the people as the body of Christ - we have changed the structure of churches. The protests over remodeling old churches

even reached legal action, formal complaints to Rome. Have these changes been successful? Have we not only brought people closer in a physical sense to the action of the Mass, but inwardly as well, to the awareness of themselves as a community being formed, as a family who know and have regard for each other?

3. That brings to mind the sign of peace. And, in many churches, the interval before Mass when people are invited to introduce themselves or greet their neighbor. Or the role of greeters to welcome people as they enter the church. All this has been mocked by some as imitating the Protestants, and caused dismay to others who just want to "drop in and pray." And remain anonymous! (But is the Mass the time for the quiet visit? Some will answer it's the only time they have.)

4. Frequent communion - indeed, the reception of the sacrament now by almost everyone - is, or appears to be, a huge gain. But does any of the old discipline still prevail - the fasting, and what the church prescribed as the state of grace? Any realistic observer knows what is the answer in the popular mind. The fast, no. The requirements for confession of mortal sin, etc., no. We need to rethink many things here, and take seriously the statement of Catholics that they feel their sins are forgiven in many ways and by different rituals.

We now emphasize the communal aspects of the eucharist. And this means not just the church as family, but the people as members of Christ's body. Look at the change in giving communion. Before the reform, the prayer which the priest said to each communicant (in Latin, of course) was: "Corpus Domini nostri Jesu Christi custodiat animam tuam in vitam aeternam."

("May the body of our Lord Jesus Christ keep safe your soul to eternal life.") Most people did not know the meaning. They made no answer, and received the host, kneeling and on the tongue. The shift now is dramatic. The single phrase the minister utters is "the body of Christ." And the answer expected? "Amen." Amen or affirmation to what? To being a member of that body.

But here is the key question: is the liturgical reform, this new and correct emphasis on the eucharist, deepening one's awareness of what it means to be a Christian? Do we not continue to need prayer, meditation, instruction, retreats, etc.? Of course we do. But the primary means, the *fons et origo,* is still the liturgy. It begins with baptism. It continues through a whole sacramental life. And now, especially through participation (inward and outward) in the Mass. One could ask this key question in many ways. Because of the liturgical reform, or at least partially because of it, are Catholics more compassionate? Prayerful? Concerned about injustice? Stewardship - think of the environment. Striving for some simplicity in lifestyle? Abandoning the mindset of racism or super-nationalism that has brought such horror into the world? Involved in the corporal and spiritual works of mercy? More than just occasional worshippers on Sunday? One is reminded of the mocking jest around in the 1960s: "If you were arrested for being a Christian, would there be enough evidence to convict you?" And once again, what should that evidence consist of? Think how we legalized the phrase, "practicing Catholic." That meant one who went to Mass, supported the parish, and in fact, kept the six commandments or precepts of the church. But what *is* the practice, if not the active works and life of love, the worship of the Father with Jesus and in the Holy Spirit, the ministry continuing through us of Christ to the world, the many ways that the kingdom of God comes, on earth as well as in heaven.

No one should minimize the enormous good works right now of Catholic communities and the official church. Catholic Relief Services across the world and Catholic Charities in our own country are hugely effective. New martyrs spill their blood; the Jesuits alone have had 46 since 1973 in Latin America. Our recent problems as church make us forget the quiet heroism and holiness and organizational effort that go on every day. A heroic Catholic layman like Dr. Paul Farmer, now called "the physician to the world," and a new martyr whose life was given for the sake of the poor in the Brazilian rainforest, Sister Dorothy Stang, may have been motivated by the gospel, not necessarily the liturgical reforms. But now the gospel is read and preached to the Catholic world at every Mass. And now we are becoming a biblical people, as our scholarship and interest grows apace. Now we receive the bread broken to share which we believe is the very life of Christ held out to us. Now we call upon the Holy Spirit to bring about the fullness of grace, all that we mean by the kingdom. With all this, should we not expect, of ourselves and others, to be more than casual believers, occasional Mass goers, and only slightly involved in the works of the church and the world? Should we not expect more committed Christians? Everyday saints? Eamon Duffy in the book cited reminds us that changing the *modus operandi* changes one's thinking or belief in the process. Is the Mass as celebrated now a casual or communal affair? Is the involvement by the people, at last, really internal, and changing us from within? (One thinks of a remark by Pope John Paul II: "You can only know me from the inside.")

The Effort to Understand

A thoughtful commentary on liturgical renewal was given by a member of the Curia, Archbishop Vergilio Noe, who was then the secretary of the Sacred Congregation of Worship. He encourages special studies but urges a parallel popular education for priests and laity who can't go away for Ph.D. work. (How much are we doing at this level in the parish? Does the parish pay for a good library? Does it bring in speakers, send people away to conferences, exchange homilists and celebrants?) He insists that "it is necessary to get down to the painstaking, constantly absorbing work of understanding the liturgy" and not be content with merely making some surface adaptation. He quotes a passage from *Insight,* by Bernard Lonergan: **"To strike out on a new line and become more than a weekend celebrity calls for years in which one's living is more or less constantly absorbed in the effort to understand."** A forceful remark; it reminds me that if one comes slowly to a new understanding of the scripture based on sound scholarship, it is necessary to do more than "dump it out" in a homily. For instance, it is a challenging task to wean people away from fundamentalism, which is still widespread. But to understand the power of myth and story in scripture (and in all religion), to see how deep, universal truth is conveyed is an exciting discovery - and must be shared. To understand the resurrection in its full context of Jesus' lordship, a power to renew all things, and a presence that is so much more than some miraculous vision or apparition, is another "insight" that must change one's spiritual life, not just provide a new departure for a sermon. The archbishop says, "The truth is unchangeable, its expression is subject to change." That is hardly new; Pope John said the same about the substance of faith. But we are just beginning to come up with the right expression for our age. When he adds, "The only unchangeable text is the word of God" one is prompted to ask which translation and which exegesis.

The Lonergan quote is right to the point. In my preaching since the Council I have indeed followed the urge to strike out on a new line - many lines, e.g., the place of joy, not superficiality but joy like the deep river - in Christian life. Or the right understanding of sexuality. Or the greatest challenge to belief, which is, of course, the suffering of the innocent, the problem theologians call theodicy. And the resurrection: the manner in which a community of faith, writing long ago the gospels that come to us under a single name try to share their understanding of Jesus with us today.

"The teaching given in the liturgy is more accessible to the faithful than a course of study; the liturgical books are the Church's theological books." I am not sure this guide is always adequate; Pentecost, for instance, has never been well communicated despite the rank of the feast (equal to Christmas and Easter), and the role of the Spirit is often not developed in the eucharistic prayer as one might wish. Nor will "the concept of sanctity as seen in the Masses for the saints," while helpful at times, always speak to our times. How much we need "latter day saints," to understand the life and witness of some of them not yet canonized – like Dietrich Bonhoeffer, Dorothy Day, Cesar Chavez, Helder Camara, Oscar Romero, Viktor von Hugel, Pat and Patty Crowley, the Jesuits and their companions in El Salvador, Sister Dorothy Stang in Brazil. And many more.

He calls for artistic excellence. But it isn't true that "the Church has always encouraged artists." At times, yes, but there has been little of the suggestion that follows: **"Musicians must be encouraged, young people should be trained to sing and play musical instruments not only for the inherent value in this but for the service of the community. It must be remembered that music, art and architecture are not secondary matters; they are precious instruments for communicating the message of salvation."** Often they *are* secondary. We buy a poor electronic organ for a church that cost a half million. Or we design a church that turns out to be a poor sounding box or is built in the standard "shoe box" design, helpful only for people who don't wish to get involved.

He reminds us of the great pioneers in the American liturgical movement, people like Virgil Michel and Michael Mathis, and asks who is replacing them. He strikes a note of realism which could sound pessimistic: "There are moments when, as we look back, it appears that although all has changed yet nothing has changed." Why? He thinks that opposition to the change was relatively small but the catechesis was perhaps insufficient.

I think sloth is one of the reasons, and a common view that religion should validate or legitimate one's way of life, not call it into question. A major example: our individualism that often runs counter to the emphasis on the need for community. But all this means that our work is not done; he calls for a "neo-liturgical movement" and affirms that the aim is still "to build up true communities of faith which are able to articulate that faith, to witness and to act."

Lonergan's words suggest to me that we should not be afraid of newness. How much need there is to absorb through long reflection the way reality is being shaped for us by our incredible technology. The wedding of science and theology has just begun, and the convergence so far is exciting. We now have the capacity to speak of the universe in terms of galaxies, atoms and quarks, particles and waves, energy constantly assuming new forms and the interchange or communication among those forms. It is increasingly evident that we need a vast rethinking and reformulation of being, and being human, of the meaning of God revealed in Jesus, and the astonishing promises or claim that we are one, and part of the Holy, even the Eternal.

A Quiet Time?

Almost twenty years into "the new Mass," *U.S. Catholic* magazine featured a clash of opinions, beginning with an article entitled, "Bring Back Quiet Masses." The author called the old Mass a respite from a world crowded with distraction, and the new Mass an intrusion - the directions, the prayer together, the physical contact (sign of peace) and expected cordiality leaves her ill at ease; she has lost the time the Mass once gave her for private prayer. This magazine concludes an opinion piece with reactions from readers who had received the article in advance and polled for their opinion. A large majority disagreed with her and cited the usual arguments of liturgists that this is a time for public prayer, for joining the community, for meeting fellow members of Christ's body. They reminded her that the Last Supper was not a quiet time. But one said, "Three months of hand-shaking and love talk, and no one has made any effort to become friends." One correspondent observed, thinking of St. Paul's description (*I Cor 11, 17-26*) that "Masses in apostolic times were kind of a potluck dinner party!" True enough for a while, but the practice of having a meal before concluding with the eucharist had faded by the end of the first century.

Her letter illustrates a failure of church leadership in reaching and forming people. Temperaments differ, and the suggestion to find other times for private prayers runs into the hectic life so many lead. The Mass in the past was an hour (and often just a half hour) when there was more or less silence, no directions, a lot of kneeling - and a handful receiving holy communion.

Latinists and the Old Rite

A report in *The Tablet* (6/28/03) on the Tridentine Mass is revealing. The "Old Rite" draws no great numbers but enthusiasts from a wide spectrum. There is even a religious society, The Fraternity of St. Peter, with two seminaries (in Germany and Nebraska) committed to the pre-Vatican II Mass. These people are in communion with the church and should not be dismissed as retrograde ultra-conservatives, etc. There are many other Latin enthusiasts who are schismatic, such as the followers of Archbishop Lefebvre (the Pius X Society), and the producer of the film on the Passion, but they reject the whole of Vatican II.

We have needed better teaching on the history and meaning of the liturgy. One of the excited devotees of the Tridentine rite called it "the Rolls Royce" of Masses, the Mass of the apostles, a work of art that great composers had enhanced with their masterpieces. The apostles, of course, knew nothing of this. In introducing the new rite, Pope Paul VI said that we have rediscovered the history and understanding of Mass in the early centuries, and this is reflected in the reform.

It is moving to read the testimony of Justin Martyr as to the way Christians worshipped at the end of the first century:

> **On the day called Sunday, all who live in cities or in the country gather together to one place, and the *Memoirs of the Apos-***

> ***tles*** **or the writings of the prophets are read, as long as time permits; then, when the reader has ceased, he who presides gives a verbal instruction, and exhorts us to imitate these good examples.**
>
> **Then we all rise together and pray, and... when our prayer is ended, bread and wine and water are brought, and he who presides in like manner offers Eucharistic prayers and thanksgivings according to his ability, and the people assent saying, "Amen."**
>
> **And there is a distribution to each one, and a sharing in the Eucharistic Elements, and to those who are absent a portion is sent by the deacons.**
>
> **And they who are well-to-do, and willing, give what each thinks fit; what is collected is deposited with the president [bishop] who succors the orphans and widows, and those who, through sickness or any other cause, are in want, and those who are in bonds, and the strangers sojourning among us, and in a word, takes care of all who are in need.**
>
> **Sunday is the day on which we all hold our common assembly, because it is the first day, on which God made the world; and Jesus Christ our Saviour on the same day rose from the dead.**
>
> **And this food is called by us the eucharist... Not as common bread and common drink do we receive these, but ... we have been taught that this food... is the flesh and blood of that Jesus who was made flesh.**

All this was eucharistic worship. Is it not still what we do today? As for the great composers giving us their Masses, they have indeed given us incomparable works of art inspired by certain texts of the Mass, by no means all of them, and in every case omitting its most central theme of offering and receiving. Where the classical Masses are still used in actual liturgies they are now combined with participatory rites and prayers by the people. Listening indeed is participating, and great beauty is a way to God. But the self-gift of God in Jesus, and then the gift Jesus made of his life and death, and now, of Christ in us making the same self gift with the help of the Holy Spirit - and all to the glory of God the Father – this is the heart of what we are doing.

We are further told that facing east is the traditional and symbolic position, directing us towards God, and that the new Mass is people-centered, in danger of worshiping not God but the people. So much for all these years of praying and saying, "The Lord be with you" and answering, "And also with you." (Or, "And with your spirit.") So much for the meaning of baptism and adoption, grace, and divine immanence. And Genesis telling us we have God's life within, and are made in the divine image. Do we *ever* get across these fundamental concepts? Yes, there can be a danger of thinking ourselves not as servants or Christ-bearers but as performers, liturgical stars, pop artists, etc. Any human act can be corrupted, and we need constant reflection or review on what we are doing.

"Facing the east." "Worshiping the people." Yes, the Muslims face Mecca. And east and sunrise are good symbolic reminders of the Light that came into the darkness. But nothing - nothing - is more important than developing a God-awareness or Christ-consciousness among people we baptize in the name of the Trinity.

One critic of the new rite refers to a priest who rips it off in ten minutes. Come off it - talk to any really older Catholic about the travesty of time and reverence in the not-so-good old days. Today, with any decent celebrant and with a competent parish and liturgy committee, the daily Mass is a half hour, including a brief homily or introductory remarks, and Sunday Mass is, at last, a full and gracious hour, even more upon occasion.

At the Tridentine Mass held each week in a London parish they give no sign of peace (it's considered "terribly distracting"). Announcements are made that communicants must be in the state of grace, fasting for one hour, and receive the host on the tongue. When will there be a successful catechesis that receiving in the hand is the traditional way to receive, much easier, and also - really important today - more hygienic? More details on "the Old Rite" in London: there are no lay readers and no auxiliary ministers. Any theology of lay priesthood or shared ministry is set aside for the view that the role of the laity is to assist the clergy *after* the Mass, in the parish. So it becomes, again, a totally clerical rite. No women, including girl servers around the altar. Indeed, no one around the altar except clerics and properly vested males.

The exclusion of women, we are told, has nothing to do with gender bias but comes from the role of the priest as representing Christ who in turn is the bridegroom. The altar servers, boys and men, are like attendants to the bridegroom. And the whole process may facilitate their desire to become priests. Another devotee says that people in the new Mass with ministerial roles seem to be proud of themselves. Indeed they should be.

They insist that the church is open to many rites, why not this one? And that could be accommodated. But often the real issue is what kind of theology or understanding of the eucharist is underpinning all this nostalgia and restoration.

SUGGESTIONS AND THE FUTURE

Better Prayers

The three Mass prayers by the priest (apart from the central Eucharistic Prayer) which follow the invitation "Let us pray" are far from effective. The ones provided are repetitious, and say the expected so routinely that the ear is rarely caught; attention is not focused. They are flat. The problem won't be solved until we have texts that don't come from a committee and through translation. More is needed than knowledge of scripture and doctrine. A knowledge of the human condition is needed, and above all the skill of the poet, the craftsmen of language. The rhythms of speech, the parallelisms, and the diamond-like quality of good prose are simply not present in much of what we say or try to pray. Here are the observations some years ago by a St. Louis priest, Monsignor Joseph W. Baker, writing an editorial in the archdiocesan newspaper.

> **The prayers which are used in the celebration of Mass should be the best that man can devise. They should inspire and encourage us and lead us to a deepened perception of our relationship to Almighty God. In point of fact, the variable prayers of the Mass - the opening prayer, the prayer over the Gifts, and the prayer after Communion - are usually bland, often insipid. This is not a failure of God, who has committed the eucharistic banquet to the Church. It is a failure on the**

part of those who translated and prepared our revised liturgical texts. When was the last time that any of us felt uplifted or moved by the opening prayer of the Mass? The purpose of the opening prayer is to introduce us into the spirit of the liturgy for the day. How often does the opening prayer reflect the scriptural lesson to be found in that day's readings? How often does the opening prayer draw us into the spirit of the feast of Our Lord, of the Blessed Mother, or of the saints, or seasons we happen to be observing?

From the beginning of the homily service *Good News* I sought to answer that need by preparing for each Sunday new presidential prayers for the Mass. And other prayers. All this was gladly accepted by some. On one occasion I traveled from Boston to Weston, Vermont to join the crowd at a Sunday Mass offered at Weston Priory. The liturgy there had become a prime example of simplicity, beauty, hospitality. The monks made a barn into a well-appointed chapel, but the crowds grew so great that the barn was opened up and they sat on the hillside. A gospel scene. It is not easy to find Weston and we were late, arriving just as they were singing the preface. It was one of mine, the Preface for Spring. I have written many prefaces, not only for the liturgical year but for temporal seasons, to emphasize that we give thanks for all the gifts of God, most of all for Jesus Christ but also for creation, the primary gift of the earth.

But how have I done all this – legally, rubrically? Strictly speaking, I couldn't. But I relied on priests to make a pastoral judgment, as I did, that the need to pray well allowed a stretching (or ignoring) of some rubrics. It is the "Sabbath is made for man" approach, and one that relies on the spirit, not the letter of the law. It is unconscionable to find a weekday preface for Mass that says, "In goodness You created man; in justice You condemned him." This is the old take, of course, on Adam's sin. When do writers of liturgical texts catch up with our biblical scholars?

The weakest of the presidential prayers are the few words said over the gifts, and the post-communion. It is exasperating to find that one is saying but not really praying pious thoughts in well-worn phrases, next to nothing of memorable prose. For the Prayer over the Gifts I repeat often the words from the epistle to the Hebrews; they are from a psalm (*Ps. 40: 6-8*) and applied by the New Testament author to Christ: **"As Christ came into the world he said, 'No offering, no sacrifice was your demand. You have endowed me instead with a body. See, then, I said, I come to fulfill what was written of me where the Book (the Torah) lies unrolled: to do your will, O my God, to do your will'"** (*Heb. 10: 5-7*). Why the frequent repetition? To grasp what is being said here is of great importance. It is one more reminder that rites must lead to righteousness. All liturgy is like the raft, in the teaching of the Buddha, that is abandoned when one reaches the other shore. (We often don't reach "the other shore" in a noisy, disorderly or poorly done liturgy.) And all worship must help us to seek the kingdom on earth as well as heaven. I incorporate a similar text into the baptismal liturgy; it is the well known text from Micah: **"What is it that the Lord requires of you, but that you do justice, love mercy, and walk humbly before your God."**

The post-communion prayer should be one that aids meditation, after the prescribed period of silence. If the presider remains seated and omits the invitation, "Let us pray," the people will also remain seated or kneeling. (We have too much of what is mocked as "holy gym.") A presider should be able to compose a prayer that reflects the scriptures and teaching of the day (or use one from someone who can). An alternative is to borrow from the treasury of great prayers; people will come to know the Good Shepherd psalm, the St. Francis prayer for peace, the passage from St Ambrose that begins "In Christ, then, are all things, and he is everything to us." And many more. Poetry - and beauty - belong very much in our liturgy.

Some Rituals to Improve

The Responsorial Psalm. The refrain (a psalm verse alternated by the congregation with the cantor's singing) is often not caught when announced, and the rehearsal before Mass can be ineffective. Although the prescribed choice of psalms attempts to reflect the readings, often it does not work out well as prayer. The cantor is singing words we often don't get, and expecting a response we often don't give. The celebrant may sit there mute. The liturgy planners could choose four or five of the best psalms and use them alternately for long periods of the church year. The choices? Obviously Psalm 8, on creation. Part of Psalm 139, with its great sense of God within and above. Part of the *Miserere* (Psalm 50) to express repentance (skipping the horrid line, "in sins did my mother conceive me"). Psalm 22-23, of course, the Good Shepherd. There are others, but make five or six of them prayers so familiar they can easily be sung without a book, and throughout one of the liturgical seasons (how many psalms could someone right now recite or pray by heart?). Another alternative: the Magnificat, and other Marian anthems.

The General Intercessions (Prayers of the Faithful). This was an innovation with the new Mass, and seems like pure gain, because the people participate, the answer is easy, and so on. But often it works poorly. If one asks for petitions, which is practical only in small or daily Masses, some people "take over" with weary regularity. One solution: just ask people to call out the first names of the sick and the dying. God knows us each by name. Add a short prayer for healing; St. Augustine's beautiful prayer is apt: "Watch Thou, dear Lord, with those who wait, or watch, or weep tonight...."

Another approach: some churches prepare a book for petitions, available at the rear of the church. Someone is appointed to read these and summarize them. Or, simply, the book is brought up to the altar and placed in front of it. The old custom during November was to pile up the altar, or shelves nearby, with the envelopes, the money removed, inscribed with the names of the dead. A new method is for parishes to maintain a "Book of Remembrance"; the family enters the name of the person now with God. The book is placed in a prominent place, inviting to prayer.

And what else? We need better models for the General Intercessions from people who know how to write well, and reflect human concerns. Some examples: "We pray for each other - for you, your family and friends, the people beside you. For the people we work with, or our classmates. For peace in our homes, and gladness in our lives."

Or, "If you are new, we welcome you to the parish (names)." "If you are leaving us, God speed (names)." And other names should be joined to prayer: those expecting children, through birth or adoption. Engagements - this could gladly replace the old "banns of marriage." "We pray for the newly married. And the newly born. And those who just joined us through baptism." Or "do you have a birthday this weekend or this week? We give thanks for you and for the gift of life." And another one: "Are you traveling, on a trip? We pray for your safe journey." In this short time we should reflect on the life, joy, and travail of people. And try to keep from well-worn or hackneyed phrasing. We should also pray, of course, for the Jews at the time of their holy days, for Muslims when the month of Ramadan begins, for Protestants on Reformation Sunday. Sometimes we swap pulpits on that day. Once we were forbidden even to enter their churches, and if allowed on some special occasion, forbidden to speak or sing - take any part in their worship. What myopia we endured.

More Suggestions

Returning to a greater use of home Masses. "Returning" because that's how it all began. And small groups of Christians now gather everywhere under various names; it is a most hopeful development for the church.

Using real bread. And made by the people. But it should be a rather flat loaf, and easy to handle -not the bulky dinner rolls I encountered in one parish.

Use red wine. Obviously a better symbol. It is required in Orthodox liturgy.

Beginning the Mass with the book (Bible or lectionary) carried aloft in procession. The cross or crucifix, yes, and candles, if you like. There is a danger of idolizing the book, which is why the church dropped "this is" from the affirmation "this is the word of the Lord." The Word is Christ, and then the word is in you. All this reminds us that bible studies should be part of parish life. Stand the book on the altar, and carry it over for the gospel proclamation.

Occasionally using another creed. This sounds dangerous, but there is another danger - of rote, non-meaning. But who would write them? St. Paul for one - several now used occasionally are from his writing, slightly adapted. And he was doing that himself - creeds already in use.

Occasionally omitting the creed. A long set of scriptural readings would be one reason.

Using the confession prayer at the beginning of Mass (instead of the alternatives). Generations of Catholics after Vatican II don't know *any* confession prayer or Act of Contrition. This one can suffice. And with a genuine time of silence to prepare, it can become a real forgiveness of sin.

Begin a practice used by the church in England, Canada, New Zealand and Australia: praying the Hail Mary at the end of the Prayers of the Faithful. It is fitting. "Pray for us sinners, now and at the hour of our death." We add the intercession of Our Lady.

Using a new eucharistic prayer. There are all kinds of cautions to be observed here, but we seem to be unaware that there are even official new EP's. Look up the approved "Swiss Canon." And use more frequently the eucharistic prayers for children and reconciliation.

Dismissing the children for their own Service of the Word. Many now do this with charming and excellent results.

Having the children present their own gifts of money. This is rather hilarious (and effective) in one parish, where even the smallest come up (usually run up) to drop in their own "children's envelope" in a special box that looks like a bank (pastors' eyes grow misty at the thought of inculcating this practice early!).

Bring the same children around the altar for the eucharistic prayer, where this is possible. And bless the little ones when they come up at communion time. Simply "may the Lord Jesus bless you." (Some argue we should give them a blessed bread. I haven't done this, but they certainly want to be part of the action.)

Commemorate so many things now ignored in many Catholic parishes. For instance, for centuries we read the so-called banns of marriage. And prayed for the dead. Nothing keeps us now from announcing and praying for those newly engaged, or just married. And nothing forbids us to call out and thank God for babies born that month, and the newly baptized. Or to rejoice in honors given, silver or golden wedding anniversaries, people newly arrived or departed. All this can be seen as a part of the paschal mystery, the constant movement from death to life. This can be done in the Prayers of the Faithful but in many instances, present the people in person or call out their names for congratulations and blessings. The crowd at daily Mass should record the day (never the year!) of their birthdays, and each should be acknowledged on that day, perhaps by bringing up the gifts of bread and wine. When I did this at one parish in Michigan it brought tears to an older person, living alone, who said that no one had remembered her birthday for so long that she never remembered a party. The weekday Mass crowd in the morning should have a coffee and doughnuts affair at least once a week. Make them a community - they should be.

Test the sound systems frequently. Ask the people, and suggest that people who do not hear well, or who wish to prepare the Mass in advance, purchase a text like the St. Joseph Sunday Missal. It covers all three years of the lectionary, and might win people away from the missalettes. For the most part, we still have a scene where the public reading is poor, and missalettes are the usual way of participation.

Use lay people occasionally to preach. You will have to juggle the rubrics or the way you introduce them, but it's being done. Call it a reflection or interpretation of the scripture.

Singing the Lord's Prayer. At least often enough so that it becomes something that can be called up at other assemblies. And perhaps a verse from a song of praise after the Great Offering.

Working towards a universal sung Mass. The embarrassment of not having one and the lack of participation at every baccalaureate Mass, high school or college, is painful.

Making copies of homilies available. This presumes they are worth printing and distributing. An updated method: putting them on the parish webpage. The homilist's name should be included.

Greeting people with music - a kind of serenade - as they approach the church on days like Christ the King or the parish feast. And Easter, Pentecost. Yes, with instruments, or members of the choir. Do it on the steps outside, not just with the organ playing inside. The same when they leave. It is a great and joyous thing that we do when we "make eucharist" and celebrate Christ's life together.

Keep (but control) the eulogy by family members or friends at the funeral. Call it, preferably, a memorial or thanksgiving. One pastor invites the remembrances to be given when the body is before the altar, just before the Mass. Why not all this at the wake? Many don't have wakes, and we want people to share the Mass. Two priests (in letters in *America*) argued that the Mass is not a memorial service but commemorates the life, death, and resurrection of Jesus Christ. Of course it does, but the Risen Christ is not just in heaven; the paschal mystery was expressed in the beloved's life.

A Book for Comments, and Our Approach to Funerals. How does our worship appear to a visitor? Or to those who share it week by week? We need to invite comments from anyone by making available a large notebook on a table at the rear of the church; here one could leave sentiments of praise or suggestions for improving. If we take very seriously this one great hour a week, we - at least the liturgical committee and the presiders - will visit and share worship in other parishes that do it well. We will seek any professional help needed, with voice, song, drama, and the artists. We would, for example, prepare well in advance for funerals. Any well-run parish already does this: some have volunteers who are there to do the readings if the family has no one, and others to be pall bearers, and - this above all - to help with food and drink afterwards. This is more than hospitality; it is an eschatological sign, the foretaste of heaven's banquet. Why should the considerable expense of the funeral meal be added to the burdens on the bereaved family? Some parishes have guilds which take turns in providing all the above, including a place to stay when relatives and visitors come. The time when death and resurrection occur are very important. In a previous book (*They Shall be Comforted*) I told of what happened in a Wichita, Kansas parish (St. Margaret Mary) when an older couple moved in who were in what we call a mixed marriage – she was the Catholic. They were childless. Suddenly she was taken ill and died within the week. Remember, they knew no one. But they had, one could say, joined a living branch of the vine which is Christ. The guild took over all the arrangements, and this kindness so overwhelmed the husband that he wanted to become part of it - within a short time he sought baptism. One is reminded of the remark attributed to Roman pagans about the new Christians: "See how they love one another."

THE FUTURE OF LITURGICAL RENEWAL

Seeking for Good Liturgy

There are parishes today where liturgy committees and an effective pastor really work on Sunday worship, where the budget includes the whole ministry of worship, especially music. These are the parishes worth seeking and joining. I know the counter-argument that people should stay and become agents of change, but in many instances this is impossible (or life is too short).

And people do go in search; it is harsh to use a business term here, but we have become "a buyers market." In the past it was said, or directed, that one should not go beyond the parish boundaries, even with such worthy objectives as hearing a good sermon, appreciating good music, or simply finding a good prayer life. There was even a belief among the laity that if you strayed afar, you could not be buried in your own parish. Many Catholics today are mobile where they can be; it is not just that they cannot stand poor preaching and poor liturgy; they tell you they need to be spiritually fed. And they seek out the churches and the pastors who make it possible. Some have even suggested there should be a directory (unofficially, of course - it would not appear in the diocesan paper!) of such vital parishes where the Holy Spirit is quite evidently at work.

A young professional person whose work caused her to travel the whole country asked me very earnestly "how to find a liturgical parish" in different cities. The best I could suggest was to call the chancery, get the worship commission, and ask - sometimes it worked. An occasional answer was "all our parishes are liturgical; they all have the Mass." True enough but she was looking for one that had taken liturgical renewal seriously. She was looking for life, not death.

I sought a response group of older Catholics who have lived through "old and new," welcomed or endured the changes. They were remarkably in favor of the "new liturgy," especially the new liturgical roles of women, but asked about the future, including ordination. They said we need to build in intervals of silence. Endure the sound level at some parish Masses, especially "family Mass" with a whole battery of instrumentalists, and you will long for peace. (But then, look at the children, the youth involved.) Intervals of silence already prescribed include a pause for reflection after the homily, and for meditation after communion. Other invitations to silence during the Mass are before prayer and after each of the first two readings but these do not appear to work out well; it comes through as someone missing their cue.

Some praised the preaching in their parishes; others despaired of it. They were quite accepting of new church buildings, even those with no pews, and wondered why the practice, which was gaining in acceptance, of standing during the Eucharistic Prayer was discontinued. There was a surprising resistance by some to the common cup, the sharing of the chalice (Christ's blood) during the communion. The objections were hygienic, and came in detail from a physician and a clinical nurse. We do need a new assessment here. During a flu epidemic a few years ago the Canadian bishops forbade sharing the cup for the same reason - the possibility of infection. The same caution should lead to making mandatory the practice of receiving communion in the hand. When the cup was first granted, the return to such deeply symbolic action surprised and pleased many, and I thought at that time - just thinking of large crowds - that it would be best to reserve it for small group Masses or special occasions, like the bride and groom receiving at a wedding, or a wedding anniversary, or the priest's family at ordination, or the immediate family members at a funeral. Indeed at weddings I have the groom and the bride communicate each other. It is a moving symbolic action.

On the other hand! The cup that is given at holy communion is a symbol of life itself. A cup is poured out, like parents who pour out their lives. A cup is emptied - so are we emptied of strength and health, by sickness and old age. A cup is filled - there are days when we are filled with high expectation, with sudden happiness. Or the cup is *waiting* to be filled, like one's life just beginning, or newly married, or starting a career. The cup is held out, in invitation. Life is held out to us day by day, inviting us to do more than exist, more than endure. The cup is broken, and lies in pieces like so many shattered dreams. Life is broken by sin, its continuity broken by death. But love has power to make life whole again. Love is stronger than sin and death. And God who is love is revealed in Jesus who said of the cup, "Take this, all of you, and drink." The cup is an inexhaustible symbol! No wonder we speak of the cup of sorrow and also the cup of joy. To share the cup in communion means we share life with all its sorrows and joys, strengthened by the divine power which is in us.

What else would I urge in liturgical renewal? Very much, *a singing people. A joyous people.* Augustine's phrase is well worn but still true: "We are an Easter people and Alleluia is our song." Add the words from another father of the church who said that "one should undertake nothing without first being gladdened by the thought of God." There are signs that this turn to Christian joy or optimism is happening. Priests and people frequently rename or refer to the Mass of Christian Burial, its official title, as "the Mass of Resurrection." This angered one liturgist who said that the Mass of Resurrection is Easter. But Easter is for good, forever. The church was right to drop the mournful chants, the tallow candles and black vestments, to bring out the paschal candle. And people are right to give up black, at least after the funeral, and the famous "widows weeds." I have one suggestion that moves in this direction of celebrating Christ's victory: it is to not only toll the church bells as people come to church for the funerals but let them peal joyfully as they leave. (Alas, some churches don't even have bells!)

Act soon upon the proposal for new votive Masses. On specific themes such as *justice, love, peace-making, forgiveness, ecumenism, ecology. And resurrection.* The people would not be dulled by texts that are repeated; they would be indoctrinated and indeed come to know the great passages by heart. Let them hear John's prologue, now lost forever in the third Mass of Christmas - hear it until they know it; in just a few verses it presents creation, incarnation, and salvation, the way to holiness. Let them hear the greatest of the psalms - for readings, not just responses. And the social justice teaching of the prophets.

In retirement centers or winter havens like Florida, often more than a hundred older people participate in daily Mass. And seniors are the majority at daily Mass anywhere. Think how much they could benefit from a series of votive Masses on resurrection, eternal life. This could really help to build a resurrection faith. And votive Masses, along with catechesis, might make us aware and involved in preventing the destruction of the earth, either from nuclear war or the damage to the environment. These are the life and death challenges we face as a world community. The late Aidan Kavanaugh, a great liturgical scholar, made the same proposal for votive Masses on themes and readings that would really fit the needs of people in religious communities. Right now we have a jumble of texts, and Masses given over to saints whose lives have little meaning for people today. They need some current examples.

One suggestion takes pondering: *could it become customary, at least on occasion, for everyone to don a special piece of clothing, a particular garment, at Mass?* Yes, I am thinking of my Jewish friends with their prayer shawls, the tefillin, and the yarmulka (what children call the beanie). It changes the look of people at worship - and changes them. What might we wear? Perhaps a stole, like the deacon stole. And why not, because it would be one more reminder of one's share in Christ's priesthood. If all this sounds too much, perhaps the wearing of a simple cross, crucifix, or other religious insignia like the fish would suffice. A well-made pendant, put on as part of the preparation for Mass. Is all this fanciful? Perhaps. We have lost the battle for "dressing up" on Sunday, and indeed, making the Sabbath a different kind of day. But these suggestions might take hold. And if they don't? Well, invite everyone to wear something red on Pentecost Sunday! Clothe the church in crimson, the sanctuary with roses. Proclaim the gospel in different languages. Use the gospel for the Vigil Mass instead of the controversial one at present. If you have the space, organize a kite festival. It is the feast of that unseen divine Power which, as the scripture says, blows where it wills. And because the Creator Spirit prompts and aids all creativity, an art festival, perhaps involving parish artists, would indeed be fitting.

Rescue, as far as possible, the sacramentals from magic. Add to the prayers; don't just sprinkle with holy water and mutter a blessing. To what end, why do you drive this car, live in this house, wear this engagement or wedding ring, say or pray this rosary, and wear this medal?

Learn from others. Quakers use long intervals of silence. Muslims especially use bodily gestures; we see pictures of the entire community (all male) bowing profoundly, head to the ground. We will not go this far! But are we too introverted (or shy) to hold out our hands when praying the Lord's Prayer? Are we too tired to remain standing for the eucharistic prayer where this is allowed? We do have gestures like the sign of the cross and the triple cross on the body when the gospel is announced. But we should keep on learning, visit other churches. We will find that Baptists really sing. Black congregations may cheer on the preacher, even vocally correct him (we don't dare to do that!). They still dress up for Sunday service. Episcopalians convey a high sense of decorum (such as escorting a speaker from the congregation to the lectern).

A major suggestion: *the need for more approved centers of experimental liturgy. And to study the liturgy.* Take this fundamental statement about the importance of liturgy from *Sanctosacrum Concilium,* the Vatican II document: "The liturgy is the summit towards which the activity of the church is directed; at the same time, it is the fountain from which all her power flows." Or add an earlier definition, from Pope Pius XII and *Mediator Dei* (1958): "The liturgy is the primary and indispensable source of the true Christian spirit." Or the old theological truism that "the law of prayer is the law of belief." Then ask how many Catholic institutions of higher learning in the United States have set up centers of liturgical study; not just graduate programs but places where problems and possibilities with the liturgy could be explored in depth, and experimental rites carried out. Places where surveys could be made as to what is actually happening, where contributions of anthropology, as well as contributions by experts on symbol and rituals, could be made, and where different rites could be experienced. How many centers are there? Four. Only four. They are at Georgetown, St. Louis, Dayton, and Notre Dame (which has led the way for a long time). We need all the insight, wisdom and expertise we can get.

Some suggestions may appear as so many nice extras. Then discuss all such changes or any ongoing renewal by engaging in serious study of the liturgy. There is a vast liturgical library that scholars have given us. Discuss the Vatican II documents (not just on liturgy but on revelation, and the church, and the church in the world). Go on field trips; learn from others.

Study, yes, but most of all, approach this with some fundamental attitudes. Worship is unimportant to many people; it must be reclaimed. It is one half of the Great Commandment! And the Mass is our greatest treasure; it has perdured even with neglect and distortion. Remember that we are increasingly an educated people, and deserve or demand quality worship, intelligent preaching. And we are also a sensory people, bodily made. Not souls with bodies but bodies with God's life. We are not angels at worship. Then appreciate how important it is to walk, process, bow down, stand as well as kneel, dance, raise hands, join them, fold them in prayer. Speak, listen, sing. Delight the eyes with good art, the ears with great sound - "signals of transcendence." We are a redeemed people - sinners, yes, but forgiven, and loved.

A Return to Trinitarian Understanding

I hope the future of liturgical renewal includes some of the suggestions many of us urge. And that authorities will listen more to people who know the history of liturgy, and the input from anthropologists, symbologists, and sociologists who can tell them where their people really are. Expressing the doctrines, even the great mysteries, in the language and customs of different peoples is necessary. But we need a recognizable rite! And it will remain for us in the west the Roman rite, but with customs and variations that come from and speak to the worshipers.

The time for all this is now. I think of the young man's response to a bishop who told him that the improvements he sought in the church would take a lifetime to achieve. The youth answered, "It is my lifetime, bishop, not yours." I have felt the same urgency about liturgical reform. We should not, right now, be using poor language and inadequate prayers in the Mass, this worship that so defines us, that engages millions every week and goes on every day. The same need for excellence means we should have better readings. If we are going to pray about God's kingdom coming on earth, and if we are going to deliver people at last from an understanding of church or God that relies on fear, much ignorance, and excessive regulations, we need to get the message right. Words do matter; it has been well said that on occasion they have the power of deeds. And the way we pray becomes doctrine (fixed beliefs, right, wrong, or inadequate) in people's minds.

A deep change in liturgical thinking and practice may well come from scholars whose objective is the right understanding - Trinitarian - of the eucharistic prayer. And consequently of Christian life. Two Jesuits have been very much involved: first, Edward Kilmartin, who left us for God in 1994 and left behind a large but uncompleted work titled, *Eucharist in the Christian West.* He bluntly says that our present eucharistic theology is wrong, very wrong. His research has been carried on by Fr. Robert Daly at Boston College. Daly has shared his work with me; he keeps it no secret and has also shared the Kilmartin approach at the annual meetings of the North American Academy of Liturgists and the semi-annual meetings of the international *Societas Liturgica.* He also took the risk of writing a popular article on the subject for *America* magazine (5/1/03) which began by saying that the popular hymn invariably used on Holy Thursday that begins, "At that first eucharist before He died," is wrong. It wasn't a eucharist.

This will startle people and take a lot of explaining, because it is certainly common belief to link the Mass with Jesus' actions at the Last Supper. Fr. Joseph Jungmann, S.J. commenting on the textual variations in the accounts of the Last Supper says that the differences probably reflect the way Christians were worshipping at the time. Before long the term "breaking of the bread" and the use of homes for liturgy had disappeared. What then? Daly notes that the Last Supper is the starting point but not the content or understanding of the Mass in the eucharistic prayers we have from the third century on. Kilmartin points out that when Jesus spoke the words we have repeated ever since, he had not yet died. Nor been raised from the dead. He had not been exalted, glorified by the Father. Nor had Father and Son made the gift of the Holy Spirit - to us, we who are incorporated in Christ. And for the Mass to be his sacrifice, the receiving of holy communion, so long ignored or even denied to the people, is essential.

The Mass is more than the sacrifice of the cross. Sacrifice indeed is offering a gift - of agapaic, sacrificial love: God to us, and we to each other. It is the Risen Christ communicated to us who is offered to the Father. Daly sees all this as coming from the very nature of God as love, which means the Trinity. In both Creation and Incarnation, this outpouring of divine love is centered on us. It gives us the cosmos, the earth and our lives. It gives us each other, and the faculties of knowing and loving; we are marvelously made. It then gives us - God. God in Jesus. In the end it does not matter that we are created in bodies that falter, fail, and die. In Christ, the new creation has begun. Jesus sacramentally (one could say truly, literally) embodies us, beginning with baptism and in every communion, so we can extend his ministry, add to the joy and lessen the pain of life. And more: enable ourselves and others to live with faith and hope. But this involves the gift of the Holy Spirit. All this is well expressed in the first part of Eucharistic Prayer IV, which says that the ultimate reason for all this divine activity on our behalf is to bring about the fullness of grace.

The Divine Love is the fountain and origin of all this. It reminds us of the great statement in the first letter of John, **"It is not that we have loved God but rather, that God has first loved us."** And in a real sense this brings eschatology - the doctrine of final fulfillment - into the here and now. Christ *has* come. We are called to live his life more fully, alert to the neighbor who needs our love, and aware of our own need for mercy and strength.

The deeper understanding of Mass may change, with better instruction. And better texts! To keep all reformers and theologians patient we should remember that people come to the holy place, for the holy deed, with different needs and desires. My own response group told me this: they come to be with Jesus. To profit from the scriptures and homily (not many say this). To pray, petition, give thanks. Above all, to be in the Presence. A few answers reflected the reform: to meet and join the community. To receive communion. To have their sins forgiven. To participate in the Mass; it is no longer just "a priest thing." All this goes far beyond older answers such as: habit, fear, church law, "to get grace." The varied response is not unusual if we remember that we are talking about a great variety of people, and ultimately of Mystery – of God, and the Incarnation.

Six centuries before Christ the philosopher Heraclitus declared, **"The gods neither declare nor hide; they set forth or make known by signs.**" That profoundly underscores what we mean by revelation, incarnation and sacramentality. The signs in my life were many, and they all pointed to the realm of grace, or God. "Being that lets us be." Love that enfolds and delivers us. Early on I discovered the Good Shepherd psalm was "sacramental." *"He brings me to waters where I may rest... he prepares a table before me... he anoints my head with oil."* I share the psalm sometimes as a post-communion meditation. It is likely that Jesus prayed this psalm - and then became what he prayed: the Good Shepherd. Yes, and holds out the last promise which we should anticipate with great joy: *"I shall live in the house of the Lord forever."*

Deo Gratias